Confessions of a Conservative Evangelical,
Second Edition

To the memory of my father
Harold Glen Rogers

Confessions of a Conservative Evangelical,

Second Edition

with a New Preface by the Author

JACK ROGERS

Geneva Press
Louisville, Kentucky

Scripture quotations from the Revised Standard Version of the Bible
are copyright, 1946 and 1952, by the Division of Christian Education
of the National Council of Churches, and are used by permission.

Cover design by Jennifer K. Cox
Book design by Dorothy Alden Smith

Second edition published by Geneva Press
Louisville, Kentucky

This book is printed on acid-free paper that meets the American
national Standards Institute 239.43 standard. ♾

PRINTED IN THE UNITED STATES OF AMERICA

01 02 03 04 05 06 07 08 09 — 10 9 8 7 6 5 4 3 2 1

Library of Congress Cataloging–in–Publication Data is on file at the
Library of Congress, Washington. D.C.

ISBN 0–664–50239-3

Contents

Preface to the Second Edition

The first book I published, after my dissertation, was this one. That was twenty-seven years ago. I was forty then, and just beginning my career of seminary teaching at Fuller Theological Seminary. I am sixty-seven now, and, for one year, Moderator of the Presbyterian Church (U.S.A.) General Assembly. I have retired after eight years of teaching at Westminster College, seventeen years at Fuller, two on the Presbyterian Church national staff in Louisville, and ten as vice president of San Francisco Theological Seminary. Upon rereading this book, I was gratified, and somewhat surprised, to discover that I am indeed the same person with much the same attitudes and ideas as I was when I wrote it.

At a few points it bears the marks of the times and my limitations. I use "man" to refer to women and men, something that changed when I served on the UPCUSA task force on Language About God from 1973-1975. Some of the illustrations refer to people and events that are no longer of current interest. It is an early attempt at narrative, or story, theology. Each of the chapters is a theological essay set in the context of one or more of my life-shaping experiences.

Writing the book was an essay in self-criticism. I struggled with my uptight, conservative background, seeking to be more biblical and evangelical, and I invited others to join me in that struggle. I recorded how I was changing. I wanted to conserve, preserve, "hold fast what is good" (I Thess. 5:21). At the same time I did not want simply to resist change and preserve the cultural *status quo*.

The word I used to describe the direction of my change was "evangelical." At the Reformation, and still in Europe, evangelical just means Protestant. In the 18th and 19th centuries, it referred to warm-hearted Christians in the major Protestant denominations who approved of revivals. Then in post-World War II America, a group of younger Christians wanted to move away from the militant fundamentalism that had caused so much strife in the early twentieth century. Identifying with Billy Graham, they wanted to maintain orthodox Christian doctrine but refrain from two marks of fundamentalism—its withdrawal from the world and its tendency to schism in the churches. Fuller Seminary, where I began teaching in 1971, was founded to be the flagship theological training center of the evangelical movement. While I was there, Fuller Seminary took the lead in another change in evangelicalism – rejection of the doctrine of biblical inerrancy, with its claimed literalism in biblical interpretation.

The essays I wrote primarily drew on my experiences prior to going to Fuller. I recounted my conservative upbringing through college, cross-cultural experiences in Egypt and the Netherlands, doctoral studies on Scripture in the Westminster Confession, being pastor of a church with people of many denominations and nationalities, and personal growth through marriage and parenthood. Only the last three chapters touched on my experience as a professor at a large, self-identified evangelical seminary. *Confessions of a Conservative Evangelical* became a popular book among younger evangelicals struggling to find a middle way as I was. Its expressions of faith and attitudes toward social issues were seemingly approved by the larger evangelical community.

Now, many people want to deny my self-description as an evangelical. Some people who report having benefited from my teaching at Fuller now want me to repent. They believe that I have made a radical change in my theology, or even in my faith. That is why I responded positively to the suggestion from Westminster John Knox Press that they republish this slender volume. Not one word in this book, save this new preface, has been changed from the original.

My basic Reformed theological position and my evangelical method of biblical interpretation have not changed. They remain essentially the same as the theology and biblical interpretation in the stories of this book. What has caused such a negative response from many of my friends is that I have applied those principles to an area untouched before, the status of homosexual persons in the church. I did not think in 1974, and I do not think now, that one's relationship to God, nor one's theological stance, is determined by one's attitude toward a particular social issue. To be evangelical is to have a personal relationship to God in Jesus Christ, to trust the Bible as the ultimate authority for salvation and the life of Christian faith, and to want to share that Good News with everyone. To define one's theology by adherence to a particular position on a contemporary social issue is to be ideological, not evangelical.

For hundreds of years the vast majority of evangelical Christians cited the Bible in defense of slavery and subordination of women. They were tragically, hurtfully, wrong. But I would not deny that they were evangelical Christians. Some of their grandchildren learned to read the Bible in a more evangelical way and changed their minds on those issues. There are, and will be, many issues on which we need more light from the Scriptures. We do well to seek the Spirit's guidance in the community of the church, listening to and learning from one another.

In 1974, I wrote: "I feel no need to apologize for my past. Nor do I feel sorry that I am continually moving beyond it." That is still true today. I wrote of experiences that had been catalysts, helping me change my mind. My desire now, as then, is to grow as a person into "the measure of the stature of the fullness of Christ" (Eph. 4:13). I invite you now, as I did then, to join me in the struggle and the celebration.

Jack Rogers
Moderator, 213th General Assembly
Presbyterian Church (U.S.A.)

Preface

This book is not for everyone. It's for people like me. I don't know how many people there are who share my experience of being a straight, uptight, conservative Christian. From what I read, the friends I know, and the students I teach, I suspect there are quite a few.

I can't be of much help to people who are liberal, permissive, generally tolerant (except of conservatives), and humanistic. They have both problems and joys that I neither share nor fully understand. I suspect that what they may need as balance for their lives is some more stability, greater deference to the past, and concern for structures and rules. I am not addressing those people. I need to listen to them. I'm sure I can learn from them.

I do want to raise some questions, very gently, for those who are new converts to Christ from very permissive backgrounds. I'm concerned for Jesus people. I feel for disillusioned graduates of the campus militancy of the 1960's. I rejoice with people of mature years who have found Christ as the answer after decades of pursuing less satisfying goals. I don't share their experience. I don't want them to have to share all of mine. My question is: Are you exchanging not only lords but life-styles?

Is an extremely conservative life-style a necessary accompaniment of your new freedom in Christ? I think what we both need is middle ground where we can walk with Christ and one another in freedom. That's hard to find. Perhaps if we can share one another's experience, we won't have to learn everything firsthand, the hard way.

The people I feel at one with are those who are conservative. I have more rules than I know what to do with. They are usually self-imposed by my overly active conscience. I've always taken for granted that what Christians need to know has always been known and only needs to be understood and repeated. I have been so obedient to authority (and so authoritarian when I had the chance) that I have been afraid of freedom. For me as a person that has often meant expressing only a part of me, e.g., my mind but not my feelings. As a citizen of the world and of the Kingdom it has often meant withdrawing from the group rather than risking change to myself. I'm taking the risk of exposure and involvement now. I trust it will be of benefit to me. I hope it will help others.

When the material now in the chapter on "Evangelical Social Action" appeared as a magazine article there were requests for copies and reprints. One request especially moved me to undertake this expanded treatment. A seminary graduate now heading the urban studies program of a Christian college came to me. He said that his students experienced sharp conflict when they confronted the real, complex problems of the city. Their conservative Christian backgrounds had so little prepared them to deal with urban reality that they felt pushed to a choice between extremes. Either they had to turn away from the people of the city and their problems, or they had to reject their Christian faith. I want to say that this is a false dilemma. The cultural packaging in which the gospel has been taught to us may not deal with all the realities of the world. The gospel of Jesus Christ *is* adequate. The issue is hearing the gospel afresh and having the guts to apply it in each new situation.

I am changing. Changing is not the same as arriving at a new place. Words are often signposts marking a journey. "Conservative" is a good word. It marks continuity with the past, preservation of enduring values, holding on to what has been proven with time. In this sense I am still a conservative. I want to "hold fast what is good" (I Thess. 5:21). There is another sense in which the word "conservative" is used. The dictionary defines "conservative" as: "tending to favor the preservation of the existing order and to regard proposals for change with distrust." Being conservative in that sense leads to conservat*ism*. That is the sense of being conservative which has marked much of my past. That is the sense of being conservative which I want to put behind me. That is the sense of being conservative which confuses Christianity with our culture. Salvation is not found in the *status quo*. From apostolic times Christians have challenged the existing order.

I need a new word to describe the direction in which I am moving. I like the word "evangelical," because it refers to the evangel, the gospel, the *good news*. In that good news there is freedom (John 8:32), wholeness (John 10:10), and an active, creative involvement in all of life (Luke 4:18–21). To find freedom, wholeness, and involvement with the world does not mean rejecting the Christian faith. For me, it means acknowledging that I am becoming more critical of my conservatism. It means believing that I am emerging as more evangelical.

Writing this book is an exercise in self-criticism. I need to clarify the values of my past. I need equally to be honest about its weaknesses and limitations. It is more important for me personally to critique my own tradition than it is to criticize an opposing position. According to Scripture, judgment *begins* with the household of God (I Peter 4:17). Repentance opens possibilities for renewal. A contemporary chorus referring to Paul's conversion has as its refrain, "It's no sin to change your mind."

I would like to change other people's minds as well. That is, I would hope that reflection on my experience would support others in their growth struggles. I want to say to Christians who are changing: It's O.K.—you can become less conservative and more evangelical. What I want most of all is discussion, feedback, sharing of insights among Christians of all orientations. I don't want labels to constrict us, to box us in, to force us to defend. Fortunately, probably none of us are completely consistent advocates of one particular position. Some liberals can be extremely defensive and dogmatic about their particular stance. And some conservatives can be liberal in the best senses of that word: open, tolerant, progressive, generous. Granted, labels can be libels. At the same time, most of us do operate within a pattern, a tradition, a style that is somehow identifiable. My use of the words "conservative," "evangelical," and "liberal" are symbols. They are less designations of theological positions than cultural orientations. They denote group attitudes to a lesser degree than they connote individual activities. No one need put on a shoe that doesn't fit. These words are only meant as initial, inadequate introductions of participants in a discussion where we hope to get to know each other better. All can learn. And I stand to learn the most by being most involved.

I feel no need to apologize for my past. Nor do I feel sorry that I am continually moving beyond it. I know that, like all living beings, I will continue to change. I don't know to exactly what changes a continued hearing of the gospel will challenge me. This book and the response of others to it are part of the process. For me, to be evangelical is to learn from the past, to bear witness to an ever new and deepening faith in Christ in the present, and to be open to the future God has for us.

Committing myself in writing is a privilege and creates problems. I need to make clear what this book is not. It is not an autobiography. I'm not concerned that you know about my experience, except as it touches your experience. I want to affirm my value as a person in order to affirm your unique worth. I hope we can appreciate how we are different and what we share.

The chapters that follow are theological essays. But I hope that they are theology done in a new style. They express my theology as it is developing in the context of my life experience. It is my story. I want to encourage each of you to tell your own story. The Bible is full of "case studies" of real people interacting with a very real God. Most of the Biblical material comes to us in this form of theology arising from concrete life experiences. The Bible is to be a canon, a measuring rod, a norm by which to judge and direct our lives. We need to know our own story in order to compare it. Then the "old, old story" can come to life again in our lives.

This book is not meant as an enduring theological tome. As I explain in Chapter 4, for me theology is a human, trial-and-error enterprise. All of theology must be redone in every generation if the church is to be healthy. To be sure, there are guidelines and precedents and models. But because there are always new problems, there is always a need for new insights and new applications of the Biblical data. This book is meant to stimulate your thought. I hope it may encourage discussion from the right, the left, and all points in between. Nothing would please me more than to have other persons pick up the modest suggestions made here and to work with them in more substantial and creative ways. And especially if someone can find more useful, more descriptive, more helpful terms than "liberal," "conservative," and "evangelical," we will all benefit. This book is not meant to close any questions. It is meant to open the consideration of options.

This book is not an institutional position paper. I am speaking for myself. I am not speaking for Fuller Theological Seminary, where I gladly teach. Nor am I speaking for the United Presbyterian Church, whose ordination I gratefully bear. I struggle with rightful loyalties to these institutions and to others, such as family and nation. And I struggle to know and be true to myself. Of this I am sure: My first loyalty must be to God revealed in Jesus Christ. To put any other loyalty first is idolatry. In some sense, that struggle is what this book is all about.

The chapters that follow indicate experiences that have been catalysts, helping to change my mind. They are not the kind of agents that produce change without themselves being modified. An Oklahoma oilman recently taught me that experiences are like enzymes. They become a living part of you and continue to grow and develop with you. My past is a part of me. I don't want to reject it. I simply want to grow as a person into "the measure of the stature of the fulness of Christ" (Eph. 4:13). For that I need the fresh new wine of the gospel, which is continually tearing open my old conservative wineskins (Mark 2:22). I agonize and rejoice in the process. Will you join me in the struggle and the celebration?

J.R.

Acknowledgments

I wish to express my appreciation to the following friends and colleagues who have read and responded to some part of the manuscript at some stage of its preparation: Glenn Barker, Bob Coughenour, David Hubbard, Dale Johnson, Chuck Kraft, Peter Macky, Bob Munger, Jim Oakland, Lew Smedes, and Mel White. I was not able to implement all of the advice that they gave, but they have surely had an influence for good. This is my story. They each have a story of their own to tell. I appreciate their criticism and collaboration in these efforts to describe my development.

My sincere thanks go to the students of all ages in Pasadena, Hollywood, and Seattle who have read and responded to these pages as they were in progress. As forerunners of those who might later read these pages, they gave me hope and help.

Dolores Loeding deserves special thanks for typing and retyping the manuscript. She has always met even the most difficult deadlines.

My wife, Sharee, and our sons, Matthew, John Mark, and Toby, are part of me and part of this story. It does not begin to do justice to the blessing they are. They have encouraged and enabled me to express my experience. They each are living out a significant story of their own. I hope to share with and support them, as they have me, in whatever form of expression they choose.

CHAPTER 1

Where I've Been—
Sound Familiar?

I was born an American and baptized a Methodist. I became a Presbyterian by geography. My father was drafted into the Navy in World War II and we were forced to sell our car. There was a small, neighborhood United Presbyterian church just a block and a half from our corner. We continued to attend there after the war, and I grew up in that church until I left home to attend seminary.

A Conservative Church

The old United Presbyterian Church of North America was a small denomination (about 225,000 members). It was conservative, but not fundamentalist, having somehow stayed outside the liberal-fundamentalist controversy that rent another denomination, the Presbyterian Church in the U.S.A., from the 1890's until into the 1930's. (See Lefferts Loetscher, *The Broadening Church*, for the Presbyterian U.S.A. story and Wallace Jamison, *The United Presbyterian Story*, for ours.) I remember only a little about the pastor under whose leadership I joined the church when I was about twelve. I do know that he induced me to study and memorize large sections of the Bible.

The minister who succeeded him was the most decisive pastoral influence of my early life. The pastor of my junior and senior high school years was an ex-insurance salesman who had gone to a Southern, nondenominational seminary as a man of middle age and had been an Army chaplain at the end of World War II. He was rather aloof and impersonal, an efficient administrator, but above all an excellent preacher and teacher. The excellence of his preaching lay in the clarity of his thought and his mastery of Biblical detail. This was very attractive to me, and I was the only youth who regularly attended his Sunday evening Bible studies. I learned the dispensational interpretation of the Bible thoroughly. I think that its primary appeal to me was the impression that there was a grand, divine plan which encompassed and explained all of reality—past, present, and future.

A Conservative Family

My early Christian home training had prepared me for the identification of "conservative" with "Christian," which was reinforced by the church. My parents were regular churchgoers. My sister and I went with them as a matter of course. I do not remember being forced to go, nor do I recall there being any other choice. My parents were really rather modest in their expressions of piety. They said grace at meals and read from the Bible before going to bed at night. They were very emphatically against smoking, drinking, and extramarital sex. I internalized those values and was very concerned to live up to their standards—the same standards I learned at church. Smoking and drinking I shunned. While this set of standards tended to separate me from my peers as I grew older, it also strengthened my own sense of identity. Christians simply did not do certain things, and by strictly adhering to certain very clear rules I was reassured that I was on God's side and he on mine. My greatest struggles during my teen years were probably with sex. That took the form of struggling to suppress sexual fantasies rather than of any real inclination to act them out. My parents were very supportive in that they showed great confidence that I would follow the guidelines which they set. I lived, during high school and college, in a basement apartment in our house and always had my own key. I was not conscious of my parents even knowing when I came and went much of the time. My reaction was to police myself quite strictly. Both the family and the church taught me that Christians were different from other people in clearly identifiable ways. Motives, mitigating circumstances, how you felt about yourself—none of these came into the discussion. There were absolutes to be kept. I knew them, and I kept them.

Both my pastor and my parents served as models for me and taught that rational self-control was a prime Christian virtue. When my parents argued, it was always the one who kept most controlled who won. I learned that to lose one's temper, to shout or cry, was to lose the argument. To keep cool and logical was to get your way. My pastor taught me the same lesson. I cannot imagine him weeping with a bereaved family. His strength was always to be calm, in full possession of his faculties and able to give a reasoned answer. I identified with the controlled, rational approach and unconsciously assumed it to be the Christian way. The rational, well-outlined, systematic sermons of my pastor gave a framework upon which all my experience was interpreted. I certainly distrusted my feelings. The material in the Bible was treated like prescriptions from an all-wise doctor. I took these prescriptions and did my best to force my experience to conform to what I was being taught. Somehow I never really considered the opposite possibility— that my pastor's and parents' experience made them interpret the Bible the way they did. The notion that the Bible recorded the experience of people encountering God was foreign to me. The Bible was like a computer printout from on high. It contained truths, rules, absolutes, universals, all fitted into a system to be learned and obeyed. That view did not give much joy, but it gave real strength.

I was fairly miserable throughout junior high school. I had grown up in a predominantly female neighborhood and my parents frowned on athletics as too rough and not worthwhile. Although I was physically able, I was not experienced enough to make organized team sports when they took prominence for my peers. In senior high school I began to find my niche in verbal and organizational activities. I excelled in debate and was elected to the student council. The first time I kissed a girl it was because my role in a high school play required it. I played in the band and was developing an ability in track. In my senior year the cherished hope of athletic achievement was almost mine. I was invited out by the coach and given a uniform. But I soon dropped out with an injury to my knee. I went to the doctor against my parents' wishes (they didn't consider it serious). The doctor confirmed what I had guessed. The injury rooted in the fact of some calcium deposits on my knee caps. I believed, but did not tell him or others, that the genesis of those calcium deposits was in the hours spent each day kneeling in prayer on a damp cement floor in my basement room during those high school years. I didn't consciously blame God, nor change my devotional practices. All during high school and college I read a chapter of the Bible and spent at least an hour in prayer morning and evening. Just at the time of my track disappointment I was invited to give the commencement address for my high school class. I did it and received much praise. I felt that God had rewarded my faithfulness.

Conflict in College

My college years were ones of strong reinforcement both of my religious world-and-life view and of my generally distant way of relating to people. I declined to join a fraternity although I received numerous bids and most of my high school friends joined. I couldn't give allegiance to a group whose values (especially drinking) I didn't share. I didn't want to be tempted to change my standards and preferred to remain apart as the safer course. I lived at home and commuted to school. My Sundays were spent in home church activities and in rest and quiet Bible study and prayer. I never studied on Sunday during four years of college. Only a very few times was I prevented from attending church.

Debate was my chief collegiate interest and activity. It taught critical thinking, organization, and techniques of research. The others on the team were mostly pre-law or pre-ministerial students. The coaches were two bachelors, and one of them, an agnostic, was particularly influential. We discussed religion as well as politics at length. I must have been somewhat influenced by his generally liberal views. But primarily those discussions gave me extensive practice in defending my own, more rigid set of values. I got my real college education not from certain courses but from three or four great teachers. They were all more liberal than I was. But they were all deeply interested in religion and demanded that I be able to articulate and defend my views. In college I became a defender of the faith. The more my views were challenged, the more rigid I made them and the more elaborate became my defense.

I didn't spend much time studying in college. I became increasingly involved in campus politics because I felt that Christians should be involved as individuals in effecting reform. My efforts were bent toward making rules to institutionalize and enforce moral and just behavior in student affairs. One of my favorite targets was the YWCA, whose generally liberal stance offended me. I lectured to them, and I took credit for preventing them from electing a Jewish girl (a long-time friend of mine) as president. In my senior year I was elected president of the student council and was tapped for the campus senior men's honor society. In my state, election to this society was reputed to be the door to success in business or professional careers. I worked to bring about structural and value changes in that organization and then resigned after several months, believing it to be irreformably corrupt and self-serving. That resignation was roughly equivalent to a cardinal leaving the pre-Vatican II Roman Catholic Church as far as people in the state were concerned. Professors pleaded with me to reconsider. Newspapers interviewed me and editorialized on the significance of my decision for the university. I discussed the situation privately with the chancellor of the university and felt on intimate terms with him. In many ways I was very lonely. I knew many people but didn't have time for real friends. My religious convictions reinforced my experiences and gave sanction to my individualistic attitudes. At the end of my senior year I was elected to Phi Beta Kappa. College was a success.

During college years my home church remained the center of my religious training. There were few young people in the church, and almost none of my exact age. Therefore I was responsible for organizing most of the youth activities which did take place and I was the primary youth representative of the church when that was called for. My first experiential awareness of the church beyond my local congregation came at a National Youth Convention of the old U.P. denomination. I first attended during the summer after my senior year in high school. I continued to attend each summer during my college years. There I met ministers and attractive and capable youth from all over the country. The convention was an interesting combination ·of study and political organization which suited my interests well. I won a national Bible-reading contest and was once nominated for president of the convention.

I had entered college with the idea of going on to law school. After that I envisioned a career as a Christian politician. Because of my pre-law orientation I concentrated on public speaking and philosophy courses. I also took an introductory accounting course as a recommended practical preparation for law school. I nearly failed that course. It was the only academic near-failure of my life. I either couldn't or wouldn't do the work because it completely and utterly bored me. How much that course had to do with it I can't say, but I began to think of switching my vocation to the ministry. The decision came to a head during the Christmas vacation time in my sophomore year. I spent long periods in prayer and meditation. I counseled with my pastor, and his advice was: "Don't go into the ministry if you can be happy doing anything else." That did it. I decided I couldn't be happy doing anything else. I realized that my dominant motive for going to law school was to use the law to reform society. My religious training had taught me that society could only be reformed by transforming the people in it. Thus I felt called to the ministry and saw that vocation as a way to fulfill my personal calling from God to change lives. Having grown up in a Christian home and an unemotional church, I have no point in time which I can look to as the time of my conversion. I rather look back knowing that there was a birth because I am now aware of being a child of God. But I know when I decided to go into the ministry. At a certain moment I got up off my knees and went into my parents' bedroom and announced that I was going to be a minister. The conviction of that calling has never left me. After that I planned to attend the United Presbyterian theological seminary as a matter of course. There my earlier convictions went unchallenged. Instead they were reinforced and given more intellectual form.

The autobiography I have given is meant to show that "conservative" and "Christian" were really identical for me. Attitudes that political and social conservatives would share and approve I identified as Christian in origin. My attention was on absolutes. Philosophical absolutes gave answers in the realm of thought. Moral absolutes were woven together into a rationally ordered system of thought and life. There were clear and authoritative answers for everything. I don't believe any less in absolutes now. But I am far more sensitive to my own difficulties in knowing them and my own biases in applying them.

An Idealized Self

I shared some of this autobiography with a Christian friend who is a psychologist. He suggested that I read psychoanalyst Karen Horney's *Neurosis and Human Growth* (Norton, 1970). I was startled and chagrined at how well her first chapter, "The Search for Glory," described me. Unwillingness to accept ourselves as we are can lead us to endless striving to become an idealized self. I could have defended that as proper Christian procedure. Are we not to deny ourselves and become like Christ? The difference—Horney contends—"between healthy

strivings and neurotic drives for glory is one between spon-
taneity and compulsion." I had to admit it. I always was forcing
myself to do what I thought I ought, not what I freely wanted.
Even that I could have defended as necessary. Then I was
arrested by Horney's symbol of the neurotic search for glory—
the story of the devil's pact:

> The devil . . . tempts a person who is perplexed by spiritual
> or material trouble with the offer of unlimited powers. But
> he can obtain these powers only on the condition of selling
> his soul. . . . The temptation can come to anybody,
> . . . because it speaks to two powerful desires: the longing
> for the infinite and the wish for an easy way out. (P. 39.)

That was my temptation! It is the way of the Pharisee: Continually strive to be the idealized self. And when you know deep
inside that you are not ideal you claim to be so by pointing to
your keeping of the rules—man's rules. Christ rejected the easy
way out. He refused to become the idealized Messiah, leaping
off the Temple, and making stones into bread. Christ rejected
the idealization because to accept it would have meant to deny
his unique personhood and mission and become instead what
someone else—the devil—wanted him to be.

Our churches, of whatever theological orientation, have
often been more conservative than evangelical in urging us
always to strive for the idealized self. The gospel, the good
news, says that Christ justifies the ungodly, the non-ideal. It is
to be evangelical to know that God accepts our real selves for
Christ's sake. He wants us to grow and develop the real, unique
person he has created us to be. Pharisees must live by the law.
Only sinners can accept the gospel of grace. I was conservative
in striving for the idealized self and denying my real needs and
limitations and desires. I want to be evangelical and hear the
gospel as it applies to the whole me!

An Idealized Bible

I needed an idealized Bible. I'm deeply concerned with attitudes I have had that enabled me to ignore the Bible's human character while defending its divinity. One-sidedness either way has always been recognized as heresy by the church. If we unconsciously bring unbiblical presuppositions to Scripture, we may distort its message even when we correctly quote its words. It is like Mark Twain's criticism of women's cussing: "They can get all the words right and still miss the music." We must beware of demanding that the Bible conform to abstract idealizations which suit our conservative culture. To have an evangelical view of Scripture is to accept the whole Bible as it really is—and it is a very human book of real human beings' experiences with a real God. The divine saving message—the gospel—is recorded again and again in real ways that offend our idealized notions of what its form should be. I can no longer be conservative and talk about what the Bible must be, or ought to be—reasoning logically from some idealized human notion of perfection. I want to be evangelical and accept the Word that God has given me, with all its magnificent surprises in both content and form.

An Idealized World

Finally, I tried to create an idealized world. That idealized world is a neat one of two compartments—the sacred and the secular. The idealized Christian self with his idealized Bible tries to live in the idealized spiritual realm and shut his eyes to the reality he lives in. I know. I've done it. This idealization of the world allows us to be individualistic and ignore our solidarity with all persons in a very mixed world of good and evil. Fundamentalism hardens that individualism into a doctrine of separatism and imagines that we can withdraw from reality and remain pure. Neither conservatism nor fundamentalism can accept the one, real world of which God has made us a part. Neither really hear the corporate context of the Biblical message. Our Lord underscored the Hebrew notion that salvation affects body and soul, the whole person and his place in society (Luke 4:18–22). To be conservative, as I have been, is to relate to an unreal world where injustice is supposedly healed by calling for renewed individual ideals. That conveniently ignores the real world where all I am and do affects the poor and the captive with whom I am involved in countless ways. I can no longer be primarily conservative and relate only to the idealized world of absolutism, idealism, and individualism. I need to be increasingly evangelical and accept both my corporate guilt and my shared responsibility. The good news is that we are not alone. We are members of the body of Christ, now, in this real world. To be evangelical is to learn to live out what corporateness in this reality means.

Chapter 2

Culture Shock

I didn't attend my own college graduation. While my classmates were trying to get the folds of their academic gowns to hang just right and unfamiliar mortarboards to sit securely on their heads, I got up, put on a pair of faded blue denims and a red sweat shirt and was dressed for the day. While my friends were viewing, perhaps for the last time, the familiar sights of the campus I was gazing at the great heaving swells of the mid-Atlantic Ocean. I was six days out to sea from New York —bound for France and eventually Egypt.

The Work Camp in Egypt

My denomination had commissioned eleven American young people (six fellows and five girls) to participate in a work camp in Egypt. There we joined twenty college-age Egyptians, an American work boss, and Egyptian and American codirectors to become a unique experiment in international relations. The idea of volunteers giving manual labor at a work camp was not new. It began in 1920 with a French pastor who urged students to repair the damage of World War I. But this idea was new in Egypt. We were the first significant coeducational venture of the Coptic Evangelical Church. At that time Egyptian young men and women didn't mix socially except under supervised family conditions. Arranged marriages were the accepted norm. Imagine the surprise of our Egyptian boys when an American girl called out to one of them: "Hey, cutie, come here and help me carry this." Furthermore, persons with education were traditionally forbidden to engage in any form of physical labor. At the revolution of 1952 all class distinctions were officially abolished; but as with any long-practiced tradition, its effects still persisted. The Egyptian young people had not experienced the "dignity of labor"—nor, for the most part, had we. As for the idea of working eight hours a day in the desert sun—everyone said that was crazy! We lived in tents on a narrow strip of desert beach ten miles west of Alexandria. To avoid the worst of the heat we got up at 5:30 A.M., took a nap after lunch, and worked until 7:00 P.M. to get in our eight hours. The heat of the sun was made endurable by the stiff breeze blowing in from the Mediterranean Sea. The sun, the wind, the work, and the unfamiliar food and water kept sick bay populated with guys and girls suffering from dysentery and heat exhaustion. Despite all of this and the primitive tools with which we worked, a foundation appeared and the walls of a concrete-block dining hall began to rise—the first of a group of buildings for an evangelical conference grounds.

Cross-cultural Communication

Our other problems were mild compared to the problems of cross-cultural communication. The Egyptians spoke excellent English. It wasn't the words that were a problem, it was the meaning, and the milieu out of which the meaning came. In the first place, Egyptians, like most Near Eastern people, are to our minds excessively polite. They are less concerned to answer a question than to answer it in a way they think pleasing to their questioner. Anything less would be unthinkably rude. One of our American guys, named Punch, developed a standard polite response to their flowery language. In reply to any salutation he would say: "And may your bath water always smell like jasmine!" That seemed to do the trick. The Egyptians graciously took it as a joke.

One notable instance of the communication problem sticks in my mind. The Arab sheikh from whom we were renting the buildings that we used for dining hall and sick bay visited us. He announced that he would present us with a feast. The time was set for noon the following Sunday. We asked what we should do in preparation. He replied grandly that we were to do nothing. He would take care of everything! On Saturday night, the Egyptian girls began to make normal preparations for Sunday dinner—getting out the olives, slicing carrot sticks, gathering the bread, etc. We Americans reminded them of the sheikh's promise to bring a feast. They agreed that he would, and kept right on with their preparations. Sunday came. Noon came and went. One o'clock came and went. Two o'clock came and went. About three o'clock the sheikh showed up with a shriveled-up piece of lamb which he had obviously been roasting over a fire all day. The Americans were incensed! This man had lied to us! The Egyptians were delighted with the gift and expressed their gratitude warmly. You see, they understood what the sheikh had said. They didn't just hear the words as we did, they knew the meaning which those words were intended to convey. They understood the meaning because they understood the culture out of which the man's motives arose. They understood the appropriate forms of speech he used to express his desires.

On another occasion I experienced the positive side of this disinterest in time and this great desire to please people. We didn't work on Sunday. One Sunday when I wasn't in sick bay I took the opportunity of going to an Arabic-speaking evangelical church in Alexandria. Men were directed to sit on one side of the church and women on the other. At ten A.M., the announced time of the service, almost no one was there. During the next half hour people drifted in, some singing was begun, and eventually the church was nearly full. The preacher arrived and began to speak. One of our Egyptian work campers, Josef, came in and sat beside me. Being hot and fatigued, and not understanding a word that was said, I soon fell asleep. Josef woke me and proposed that we leave. I protested that we couldn't leave in the middle of the service, to which he replied: "You're not happy, why should we stay?" When the service ended, Josef accompanied me outside and asked what my plans were. I explained that I had been invited by some missionaries to their cottage on the far side of the city. They had given me instructions as to how to get there on the streetcar. Josef protested now! The upshot of it was that Josef took me to the bus, paid my fare, rode to the end of the line with me, and made sure that I arrived safely and happily at my destination. That trip wiped out his plans for Sunday afternoon. But for him there was really no choice. Friendship is more important than time. The quality of life always has priority over keeping one's own schedule.

I was teaching an introductory course in the Old Testament during the summer of 1967 when the six-day war between Israel and the Arabs erupted. Personally, I was torn with anxiety over the fate of my Egyptian friends. From an academic point of view, the war offered illustrations that made the teaching of Old Testament easy. In many ways, modern Egyptians are much like ancient Hebrews. (Modern Israelis are often immigrants from Europe and are culturally Western rather than Near Eastern.) An Arab general would thunder that he would send five hundred tanks into the Sinai desert. Everyone in Egypt and in Israel knew that he didn't have fifty tanks to send. But, to a Semite, numbers are often meant to signify quality of emotion rather than quantity of objects.

Persons in other parts of the world neither think nor express their thoughts as we do. That doesn't make their ways better or worse than ours, just different. Nor have people at other periods of history had the same assumptions or the same manner of expression that we consider standard. The cultural setting of the Bible is different from our culture both because of time and place. It is ancient and it is Near Eastern.

Patterns of Reasoning

Anthropologists contend that humankind's reasoning processes are culturally defined. All people are logical in ways appropriate to their culture. We can discern many different kinds of thought patterns. One ancient pattern employs corporate logic. In it no clear distinction is made between identity and contradiction. A person does not think of himself or herself as an individual but as a member of a tribe or family. This leads to dynamism—the notion that all things are possessed and motivated by an impersonal force. Mana, or what the American Indians called "medicine," is the inner force that makes things and people act as they do. People in many parts of the world still think in this pattern.

Another pattern in human reasoning is what we call empirical (experimental) logic. This is the famous "school of hard knocks" where people learn by doing. The late Biblical archaeologist W. F. Albright listed five great accomplishments of this empirical reasoning—didactic literature, codified law, individual morality, early science, and monotheism—the belief in one God. We admire the results of empirical reasoning in today's modern natural and social sciences.

What we call formal logic was developed by the philosophers of Greek culture. It introduced abstract thinking and the art of deduction. The classic example of an Aristotelian syllogism is:

> All men are mortal.
> Socrates is a man.
> Therefore, Socrates is mortal.

This Aristotelian logic enables us to make particular application from assumedly universally valid, general principles. A modern development in logic is symbolic logic. It reduces concepts to mathematical symbols and thus enables us to program computers to do complex calculations quickly.

Near Eastern Thought

Contemporary people use all three patterns of reasoning sketched above. But we in the West assume that the abstract Aristotelian way is the best. The ancient, Near Eastern writers of the Bible didn't use Aristotelian reasoning until they needed to communicate with Greek culture. God's revelation came to them, was understood by them, and was communicated by them in earlier, Near Eastern forms. In seminary we were taught seven general characteristics of the Near Eastern way of thinking. First, it is contemplative. Fasting gave time for uninterrupted meditation. Note Ps. 77. Second, Near Eastern thought is poetic. Anything worth saying is worth saying beautifully. Psalm 1 gives a poetic picture of a righteous man. Third, Near Eastern thought uses vivid picture logic. A Semite did not argue from premises to a conclusion. He painted a word picture, and his hearer became involved and convinced himself. When Jesus was asked questions, he typically replied by telling stories vivid in the person-involving pictures they painted. Fourth, Near Eastern thought loves symbolism. Metaphor and simile abound in Biblical language. The words of institution at the Lord's Supper use symbols related to our physical senses to speak to us of invisible realities. Fifth, there is the Near Eastern propensity for paradox. That which appears contradictory is often a sign of the divine. For example, God is both wrathful and merciful. In Isa. 45:7 God is asserted to be the author of both good and evil. Attempts to use Western logic to explain away the paradox usually result in denying one or another part of our experience of God. Sixth, Near Eastern thought demands sincerity—within the framework of fundamental assumptions about the nature of life. For instance, the Semite is obligated to be honest in his dealings with his own people, but he has no such obligation to those not under Semitic law. Finally, Near Eastern thought emphasizes religion as "the way." Religion is not an ideology, a system of thought, or a code of ethics, but a way of life in which one walks. One walks the road of life in fellowship with God if one is truly religious. Jesus announces that he is God by saying: "I am the *way*, and the truth, and the life" (John. 14:6).

Saving Message and Surrounding Milieu

The practical application for us of the above is both simple and encouraging. God has come to all kinds of people in all kinds of cultures over a long period of time. He can come to us, now, in our culture. We do not have to adopt a particular way of thinking or living to make us open or acceptable to him. Anthropologists have taught us rightly that, while all cultures are different, there are certain human commonalities that communicate across cultural lines. That is especially important for us to keep in mind as we read the Bible. The central, saving message of the Bible applies to all humans in whatever culture. God created the world. Man sinned and wounded himself and his world. God provides redemption for mankind and the world through Jesus Christ, God incarnate. That is the gospel. An evangelical wants all people to know that good news. The cultural context into which that good news originally came is ancient Near Eastern. If we want to understand in depth how the Biblical writers understood and applied the gospel, then we will have to understand the language and thought forms of their culture. That is why enormous time and energy and intelligence have been poured into Biblical scholarship.

Those of us who are concerned with theology have a different task. Our task is to take the central message of Scripture, with all the nuances that the Biblical scholars help us to understand, and translate it into the thought forms of our (in my case) Western, contemporary culture. Here and now is where we have to understand and apply the gospel. We must be very wary, however, of the temptation to insist that the gospel came in the forms of our thought or that it must somehow conform to them. (My conservative early training had implied that our Western—even American—way of thinking and living was *the* Christian way. My experience with Egyptian evangelical Christians began to correct that misimpression.) God has dealt with a lot of people before us and different from us. That ought to give us both humility and hope!

The Protestant Reformers in their evangelical concern understood this twofold way in which Scripture is to be understood. Luther talked of "the priesthood of all believers." He wanted the Bible in German, not Latin, so that all his countrymen could hear the central, saving message of the gospel in their own language. But Luther was a scholar who read his Greek and Hebrew as easily as you and I read the daily newspaper. He knew that the fine points of Scriptural interpretation, the full understanding of the cultural context in which the message came, required scholarship to understand it. The Reformers battled the Spiritualists, who thought the Holy Spirit would do their interpreting for them, just as much as they battled the medieval Roman Catholics, with whose interpretation of Scripture they often disagreed. They knew, as we must, that to be saved one needs only the simple gospel. But to grow to Christian maturity requires a lifetime of study and practice and a lot of help from our friends—scholars and teachers in the body of Christ. To care about both conversion and growth is evangelical.

CHAPTER 3

Authority
and Community

Cracks very early began to penetrate my defensive wall. I did not know it at the time, but they penetrated to the very foundation. After my first year in seminary I stayed out a year to participate in an experimental internship. This was before the time that the general public became aware of communes with a focus on Christian community. But that is what our internship was. That was not exactly what our founder intended it to be, however. In the end, the whole experience offered a near-classic example of the conflict between individual authority and communal solidarity. All the familiar tensions were there: ends versus means; goal orientation versus personal orientation; the vision of an individual versus the mind of a group.

The Idea and the Actuality

The founder of this internship was an outstanding Christian leader. If I said his name, you would instantly recognize it. His converts probably numbered in the thousands. The men who had gone into the ministry under his influence certainly would number in the hundreds. *Life* magazine once chose him as one of America's ten best preachers. He was known internationally as a conservative evangelical.

I do not want to mention his name because this is not about him as an individual. I will have to say some harsh things about his leadership, but they are not intended to criticize him as a person. He represented a style of leadership common among churchmen, a style that conflicts with the concept of community. It is with the tension between these two styles of authority that I am concerned.

Our founder had the idea of an internship for young clergy built on the medical model. In his view, young doctors followed an older, more experienced practitioner as he made his rounds. First they observed and then they practiced under his watchful eye. The idea for the internship was announced in a sermon: "For more than a decade I have had in mind beginning an internship which would train men in a sane, wise, dynamic evangelism, such as would give them practical experience in dealing with people and helping them, as Phillips says, to 'bring them to God through Christ.' " So the concept of a spiritual internship was launched. The goal attracted me when I heard of it. But so also did the announced means.

The internship was to be entirely independent of its founder. A distinguished group of clergy were recruited for a board of directors. A young minister with evangelical background, church experience, and an earned Ph.D. was hired as the director. Interns were invited to join an open experimental program. We were told that together we were to develop a program which could serve as a model for other internship experiences (of which now there are many). It was to be an open, experimental year. That attracted me. After so many years of school, here was a chance to learn by doing, and to find my own way. But the problems were built in from the beginning. The founder had spoken of the internship's director, "who will have its supervision in his hands, with (I hope) some advisory suggestions from myself." He also indicated his intention "to spend a couple of hours with the group each week myself, talking with them about their own growth, the people they are in touch with, their deeper relationship to our Lord." Those were to become memorable sessions.

Who We Were

Eight of us came as interns. We were not selected, or carefully picked. The program could have taken twelve, but we were the eight who volunteered after having heard of or read about the opportunity. We came for various reasons, I'm sure. The only reason we all had in common was a deep feeling that this was something we were called to do. We represented four denominations and a wide range of education and experience. One man had been out of seminary for two years serving as an assistant pastor. Another had just finished college and had yet to begin seminary. The rest of us were scattered in between. Two of the men were married and brought their wives. The director and his wife had two small sons. These twelve adults, two children, a dog, and a parakeet all moved into a big old twenty-two-room house that looked like something out of a Charles Addams cartoon. We were located near the center of a large industrial city, one half block from the home of the internship's founder. Thus the internship began.

What We Did

As the year began, we were taught by a succession of guest lecturers. And what a strange faculty! There was a psychiatrist, a disc jockey, an Irish cop, a lawyer, a newspaper editor. There were prominent ministers and laymen. There were guests from other countries, including a Scottish theologian and some Australian evangelists. To all these people we addressed two questions: What do you think we should know to be better ministers? What does your Christian faith have to do with the way you do your job? The answers we got were sometimes brutally frank.

After taking it in for several months, good as it was, we could not take in any more. We had to get out and do something about it. The group decided that each of us should have an individual job, and that we would share our various experiences so that all would profit. I worked with college students at a nearby city university, visited in a nursing home, and worked in a local church on Sundays. But best of all, every Wednesday noon I went to the Harvard-Yale-Princeton Club (a place where they normally would not allow a non-Ivy Leaguer like me). There I had lunch with a group of young lawyers and executives. Their common interest was the discussion of religion, although some were agnostics. I found myself stripped of all clerical authority and deprived of the technical theological language I had acquired in seminary. What I said counted only insofar as it made sense in terms of their experience and terminology. And I learned by sad experience that I needed to do a lot more listening before I did any talking.

Later in the year we traveled. We visited evangelistic meetings and seminary classes at Yale and Princeton and Harvard and Boston universities. We visited churches in Washington, D.C., and Baltimore, and we went to Iowa State College for its Religion in Life week. At these places we observed close at hand and learned from Billy Graham, Bryan Green (Graham's British counterpart), and Alan Walker (who is supposed to be the Billy Graham of Australia). We saw evangelicals engaged in evangelism, healing services, and disciplined church membership and growth.

Life Together

Beyond all these good experiences, the most meaningful aspect of the internship was our life together. I certainly had not come into the internship looking for fellowship. My first year at seminary had been one of the happiest of my life. Few of the others had come actually looking for the greatest value in the group life. We were very different people, with different backgrounds. Yet we lived as close, or closer, than most families, but without the ties that bind a family together. And theological students are no easier to get along with than other people.

We took all our meals together, twelve adults and the director's two children, around a big table. After breakfast we had morning prayers. After prayers, each man was to be in study until noon. We read the books we chose, proceeding on the principle of individual responsibility—for when we got out of seminary there would be no one to guide our choices. Once a week we were to check in with the director to evaluate our progress.

Most afternoons and evenings we had our jobs in various parts of the city, or there were guests in the house. We had open house on Wednesday evenings, when any who were interested might come and look and chat. Often over tea and cookies the conversation became more than casual.

Friday afternoons were given over to what we called "division of labor." We did the laundry, scrubbed the bathrooms, and completed the odds and ends of housekeeping. But on

Friday mornings we participated in the one activity on whose value we all agreed. That was our weekly session on the handball courts at the downtown YMCA. Swatting a black rubber ball at a wall is a wonderful way to work off steam—whether directed at yourself or somebody else.

Two afternoons a week were our main times for group discussion and policymaking. On Monday we dealt mostly with our work outside the house, getting the insight of others to help us in what we were doing. On Friday we dealt with our interpersonal relations. Or, sometimes we didn't. Have you ever been to a Quaker meeting? All our group meetings were something like that. All policies and decisions were made as a group. The director was a member of the group but made no attempt to exercise final authority. There was no agenda. We had to come to a group mind! At first I hated it. It looked as though we were not getting anything done. There was our director, sitting, saying nothing—why didn't he direct? "Let's get this show on the road" was my inner pleading.

We began to discover some wonderful things in those group sessions. In a well-arranged, fast-moving organization there are some people whose opinions will never be heard. If you take time to hear everyone out, some remarkable ideas may come that the more verbal and take-charge types of people would never have thought of. Things other than ideas came out too. Sometimes we would sit for ten or fifteen minutes in silence. Then a dam would burst in someone, and feelings of resentment, hostility, or irritation would pour forth. The silence would be turned into an uproar of challenges and defenses. We had decided—and tried—to practice as nearly as possible complete honesty with one another, and at the same time to have true Christian concern. Really you can't have one without the other. The amazing part of it was that after each blowup (and we had a good one about every two weeks for a while) God's grace would come in and we would find ourselves on a new level of friendship. Where two or three are gathered together in Christ's name, honesty can be the means toward both opening and healing.

We didn't stop there. We couldn't. We had all been building walls around ourselves all our lives, and we couldn't expect them to topple in a few short weeks. We realized that despite all the time spent in the same house we really didn't know each other very well. So we tried a weekly pairing. There wasn't much to it, really. In a sense, it was just reviving the art of conversation. Two persons were assigned to meet together once a week for an hour. No assignment was given, except "Get to know each other." And as we did, we became freshly aware that there is a reason for everything. As you came to understand another person's background and present situation you could more easily forgive the little things that irritated you. You might come to appreciate that the faraway look in someone's eyes wasn't idle daydreaming, but an indication of problems you never would have guessed.

One thing more. One Friday afternoon, one of the least talkative of the group came forth with a suggestion that rocked all of us. He said, "I'd appreciate it if each of you guys would very frankly tell me how I come across to you." For weeks thereafter, on a Friday afternoon, a man would offer himself for the evaluation of the group. This was no holier-than-thou telling a person what he ought to be like. It was not superficial advice-giving. We had been together, in God's grace, too long for that. This was straight-from-the-shoulder reaction from people with whom we had been living in intimate contact for several months. These were friends from whom we had nothing to fear. That still didn't make it easy to take. I had my turn one afternoon. I thought it must surely be more difficult to be honest with the other guy than to take it yourself. I was wrong. I must have opened my mouth ten times, but it was dry and I couldn't speak. Finally I sort of sank back into my chair and prayed a short but special prayer that I would be able to ask for the other's evaluations. And then I did. And I got them!

What is the point of all this strange-sounding experience? I think it is that we came to understand more of what the words "Christian love" mean. The distinctive word the Bible uses for "love"—*agapē*—means unselfish concern. It means that even if you don't like someone, you are willing to act in that person's best interest. But we were learning that the reality of this kind of love involved both understanding and acceptance. It meant knowing people for what they were and not trying to make them over into our image.

As a conservative I feared that the gospel of acceptance was not evangelical. Yet no concept is more central to the good news—the gospel. Think on verses such as these: "By grace you have been saved through faith; and this is not your own doing, it is the gift of God—not because of works, lest any man should boast" (Eph. 2:8–9); "We love, because he first loved us" (I John 4:19); "But God shows his love for us in that while we were yet sinners Christ died for us" (Rom. 5:8). God loves us before we are ready, or willing, or able, to love him in return. His love enables us to love ourselves and others. And we really have to work at it with all the experience and skill we can muster. The apostle Paul throughout his letters asserts that by human standards he has worked harder than anyone else; and he attributes all success to the grace of God (I Cor. 15:10). What it takes is not work or grace, but both at the same time. What God has worked in us we must work out in our relations with others (Phil. 2:12–13). As evangelicals we need to nurture our experience of acceptance as well as to affirm the fact of it.

The Conflict

Regularly on Wednesday afternoons, into the midst of this increasingly close-knit group came the founder. I don't think that he consciously meant to intrude or coerce. It just did not occur to him that people might not eagerly want to follow his suggestions. He had visions for us, for the city, for the world. He knew little of the vision which we, together, had been developing. And he didn't ask. He always had something good to say. His suggestions for action were worthwhile. But they didn't always mesh with our developing consensus. They were alien, from the outside. Tensions gradually developed. Finally the strain became acute.

We knew that the founder and the director had been having their struggles in private for some time. One Wednesday afternoon it all erupted in the open. The founder acknowledged the broken communications and said he was sorry for his part in it. He asked to hear what we had been doing and thinking. From the heart we all poured out the life-changing experiences we felt that we had been having together. It was the best time of sharing we ever had. Then the founder pulled from his pocket an air letter from overseas. It came from one of his disciples. He announced that this was a guided bombshell from God to us. He read it. It included grandiose plans for new evangelical organizations and movements in the city. We were to have part in implementing these dreams! After he finished, the founder asked us to have a quiet time of individual prayer. (Our director later admitted that he peeked while we all had our eyes closed and discovered that the founder was writing, making notes.) After announcing that we only proceed through repentance, the founder began to go around the circle asking each of us what God had said to us in our quiet time. Men answered according to their personalities. Some were contrite and felt that most of the problems were on our side. Others were more resistant to the founder's implication that this was the case. Finally one of the most quiet men in the group broke the ice completely by saying: "God didn't say anything to me at all!" All the interns laughed with relief. Then the struggle was on. The founder became angry and said that there would have to be a lot more suffering and brokenness before we could grow. We tried one tack and then another, but the group knew now that we had our own guidance from God and that it was valid for us. Finally the founder stalked out of the room in anger. That was the beginning of the end of the internship. He had the contacts with money and influence in the city. It had been his idea. But we had been a community and knew that a free and open Christian community contained the greatest possibility for our maturity as Christians and ministers.

We had one final go at reconciliation. Our founder invited the whole group of us out to a place in the country. It was the home of a wealthy parishioner. The founder was there in seclusion writing a series of radio addresses. The place was surpassingly beautiful. Deer came up into the backyard as we watched. Everyone was in casual clothes and relaxed. It seemed like an answer to prayer.

Our founder told us the story of his life as understudy to another world-famous conservative evangelical leader. It was a fantastic story as he described their triumphs and then tensions leading finally to his complete break with his master. The most amazing part was that all the way through as he described his conflict with an authoritarian leader he was describing our conflict with him. But he didn't realize it. The founder kept on talking, thinking that he was showing us how he had kept the good and left the bad of his master. And we were more and more confirmed in our belief that unknowingly he had kept both the strength and the weakness. It was this same weakness —the leader's need for absolute authority—which kept us from being free in Christ with our founder.

Models of Leadership

We lived out the conflict between two models of Christian leadership—the military and the communal, i.e., the authoritarian individual and the accepting group. Both models have their benefits. The military model, with its chain of command where authority comes from the top down, is good for emergency situations. That is what a war is—an emergency, an exception, an unnatural situation. In a battle for survival there is no time to think and debate. People must do as they are told, instantly, without reflection. The military model is good for dealing with an emergency, to meet an external threat.

The communal model is much better for personal growth, everyday living, and the development of Christian maturity. Concepts only really become a part of us when we know why we believe them, not just that we should. When we learn by experience we are committed to our knowledge and make it our own. Listening, debating, and waiting take time. Growth takes time. The immediate task does not get done as fast. But when a task is done, it will be done far better. No one of us knows as much as all of us know. Because we are all sinners, the group mind helps us realize what is God's leading and what are our individual biases. And the group can give encouragement and support in following God's direction.

Our Lord gave three years to the internship of the Twelve. Even at the end of it they hardly understood who he was or what he was doing. He could have lectured to them, had them memorize propositions, created handy laws for them to follow. But he didn't. He let them learn. He was patient with their mistakes. He trusted them—far more than we usually trust our disciples. His manner of teaching in parables was indirect. It allowed each one to test his own experience, to become involved, to convict himself when the shoe fit.

Jesus had reason to question the validity of the military model. The Pharisees knew the laws. They had the chain of command down to perfection. They were a part of it. To them, no one could be accepted by God without knowing their rules, living their life-style, talking their language. But Jesus called them blind guides. He knew that they were straining out gnats and swallowing camels (Matt. 23:24). You don't enter the Kingdom of God just by obedience to authority. Christ accepted without rebuke harlots and heavies of all sorts if they just said they were sorry—and meant it. And usually he forgave them before they even had a chance to say anything.

I learned a lot in the internship that moved me away from being strictly conservative toward being more evangelical. I began to experience something I said I knew and had received before—God's grace. Now I could *feel* that God accepted me as I am because I had known acceptance from Christian brothers. And I was in a very small evangelical way beginning to be more understanding and accepting of others.

I also learned that we all have feet of clay. Even the greatest Christian leaders do. God uses sinners, people with feet of clay, to do his work. Otherwise he would have no one to do it. But success in one realm of Christian service is no validation of a person's virtue in all respects. Just those elements of personality which God can so effectively use in public may make a person really difficult to get along with in private. That is the way real Christianity is—people's strengths and weaknesses are often opposite sides of the same coin. That is why we can always evaluate persons, institutions, experiences, on at least two levels. We can describe them as a social scientist would—what their psychological set is, how they function in a group, where their ideas come from. And after doing all that—even if the descriptive evaluation is very negative—we can value the contribution God is making through them. For example, I could believe, on good evidence, that a certain evangelist (such as Marjoe) is a fake. I could still believe that God has both converted and healed persons through his ministry. As a Christian, however, I should not naïvely accept what is phony, or vicious, or unhelpful, just because God brings good out of that evil. I am grateful that God uses sinners. Otherwise he couldn't use me. I can value God's good gifts without being blind to man's misuse of them.

I should have known this, of course. Scripture is full of the stories of people like Moses and David and Peter, who break every rule in the book and are still called men after God's own heart. And the Bible is equally clear about the standing of fainthearted spies, court prophets, and Pharisees who know all the rules, keep their noses clean, and tell the people what they want to hear. I need the Christian community, the church, the body of Christ, to help me be honest as to which model I am following. Not all authority is evangelical.

CHAPTER 4

What Is Theology?

I can identify with Abraham! The Bible says that in response to God's call he went out, not knowing where he was going (Heb. 11:8). After seminary graduation Sharee and I went to the Netherlands to do graduate study. We didn't know what we were getting into!

A New Country

The first thing that hits you is language. We had ten clock hours with Annette, a young Dutch graduate student's wife, before we left the States. That gave us the sound. At first, people speaking Dutch sounded to us as though they had a bad cold and were always clearing their throats. Beyond that, we were out of our depth. So we started to tread water as best we could. When we arrived in Amsterdam we got a Linguaphone record course, the kind with fifty lessons on eight records. We spent about fifteen hours a week for two and a half months listening to those records—and repeating after them, over and over again. At the same time I was going to class twelve hours a week, understanding almost nothing. And Sharee was shopping. We ate pork chops until she learned the word for "chicken." Then to her embarrassment she discovered that the meat store doesn't sell chicken. You have to go to the poultry market. And so it went. After our first visit in a Dutch home we laboriously wrote out a thank-you note in Dutch. What a triumph! Only much later did our kind friends tell us what we had said. At the end of a Dutch letter you say "Greetings to your family." "Greetings" in Dutch is *groeten*. But *groenten*, with one extra letter, is "vegetables." That's what we sent to our friends.

The other thing you notice right away and always talk about when you are new in a foreign country is the weather. It was terrible. It rained all the time. That's not so bad except when you're riding a bicycle as your only means of transportation. Outdoors I was always wet outside from the rain and hot and sweaty inside from riding fast. Indoors I remained wet from clammy clothes and cold from the lack of central heating. Books have been written claiming that the doctrine of predestination was invented by the Dutch to strengthen them in their battle with the elements. I half believe it.

A Unique Professor

But we came to Holland not for the country but for a man. His name was G. C. Berkouwer. He was professor of dogmatics at the Free University of Amsterdam. When I was looking for a place to do graduate study after seminary I was busy thinking of the British Isles. Those grass tennis courts beside ancient college buildings at Cambridge appealed to me. But in doctoral study in Europe, the one professor under whom you will major is more important than the university, or even the tennis courts. I asked the advice of many people. A pastor for whom I worked suggested Berkouwer. His reasons were three: Berkouwer, he felt, was scholarly, Reformed, and fair. A special characteristic of Berkouwer seemed to be that he thoroughly understood and appreciated others' viewpoints before he attempted to evaluate them. That sounded good to me. The more I investigated, the more I became convinced that G. C. Berkouwer was the theologian who could help me the most. So, to Holland we went.

I well remember the first time I attended one of Berkouwer's classes. I arrived somewhat ahead of the nine o'clock hour. At nine, the time announced for class, the only students there were four or five Americans. At about 9:10 some of the Dutch students began to drift in. By 9:15 the hall was packed with about a hundred people. At 9:20 the door flew open and Berkouwer strode briskly into the room as we jumped to our feet and stood at attention. In Europe, a professor is somebody! Quickly he prayed a brief prayer, nodded to us to sit down, and we were off.

Imagine yourself listening for forty minutes to a lecture in a language you don't understand. That is what I did for weeks that stretched into months. You may think that some of your teachers are incomprehensible, but this one really was! I looked out of the window at the ducks on the canal. I counted the bicycles piled by the lamppost in front of the door. But I couldn't help also looking at and listening to Berkouwer. He was of medium height. He had straight white hair. He squinted through extremely thick glasses. But he was excited, and dynamic! I began to hear certain words repeated again and again. One of them was *boeiend*, which means "fascinating." Everything about theology fascinated Berkouwer. His enthusiasm was catching. After listening to him, you wanted to grab the nearest theological book and devour it.

Talking to him was even more stimulating. All examinations

were oral. You work on a subject (whatever subject you choose from your program) until you are ready for the exam. Then you apply to take it. Since Berkouwer had no office at the university he gave exams in his study at home. I remember being ushered trembling into a large room whose walls, tables, desks, and even chairs were completely covered with books. Professor Berkouwer apologetically cleared off a large overstuffed chair and offered me a cigar. He began by inquiring with real sincerity about my personal situation. "Do you have an adequate place to live? . . . How is your family? . . . Do you have enough money to continue your studies?" Gradually he drifted into a discussion of what I had read. Gently, informally, but exceedingly thoroughly, he began to move through the list of twelve or thirteen books I was supposed to have mastered. He would start with main themes, always probing ("Do you understand the problems?"). He would let me lead from strength and show what I knew. Then we moved further and deeper, down to the footnotes, till we came to my limits. Then quickly we moved on.

Just as I was breaking into a good sweat, Mrs. Berkouwer, a pleasant, grandmotherly woman, came in with a cup of coffee. She too was interested in me and my family. I'm sure I seized on that helpful interruption and tried to extend it as long as possible. But gracefully, before I realized it, she was gone and the exam continued. Suddenly, it was over. "That's fine. That's enough for today." That is all I ever knew about how I did. There were no grades. If the professor doesn't ask you to come back for another session on that material, you can assume that you have passed. And so you go on with your work.

It is *your* work. Always we were given the impression that we were not there to please the professor, nor to learn his system. We were to understand the problems. We were to discover the various methods of doing theology. We were to make up our own minds. So I was introduced to the European idea of theology as a science.

Theology as a Science

"Science" to a European doesn't mean just test tubes and rockets to the moon. Science is the orderly, thorough study of any subject. I should have known that. In *Webster's New Collegiate Dictionary* there is a definition of "science" as "knowledge obtained through study or practice." Accordingly, a careful, orderly study of the Biblical data and a sensitive application of that data to life is the job of a scientific theologian. Just because the subject matter of theology is so exalted —God, his works, and his relations to us—doesn't make theology better than other sciences. In the Middle Ages, the church claimed that theology was the queen of the sciences. That led to all kinds of trouble. Every science is on a par. Each science is good if its method enables us to understand its particular subject matter. No one method will work for all subjects. So there are no queens in science—not in theology, not in theoretical physics. Each has its own subject and its own appropriate method. A scientific theologian works with a certain body of data—the Biblical witness as Christians understand it and put it into practice. A theologian must then develop methods for organizing this data and making sense of it for us. A theologian is not a dictator of correct doctrine. A theologian is a servant of the church. He or she points out false and unfruitful directions of thought and suggests new channels of use for the Biblical data in relationship to life.

Every scientific enterprise is based on presuppositions. All scientists make assumptions, take certain things for granted, and make unprovable value judgments. We assume that there is a real world out there, that one fact will lead to another, and that honesty is the best scientific policy. A philosopher can demonstrate that you can't prove any of those items. But nobody cares. We assume them. Things seem to work out. So we go ahead.

Augustine, a church theologian (perhaps the greatest of them all) way back in the fifth century A.D., discovered the importance of presuppositions. Augustine was a philosophy professor and had tried several of the prominent religions and philosophies of his day. All thinkers, he concluded, begin their investigations from some assumed starting point. This starting point is their faith. The faith with which one begins radically determines the interpretation that will be given to the data examined. Reason and experience function within this faith framework, which enables us to make sense of the facts we encounter.

I once had an experience that clearly illustrated this for me. I was in Dallas, Texas, on a college debate trip. My debate partner, an engineer, wanted to see a newly built radio tower, the highest in the area. Another student, majoring in economics, and I went along. We rounded a corner and all saw the tower at the same moment. Simultaneously we each uttered an exclamation. The engineering student said: "What an engineering masterpiece!" The economics student said: "How much do you suppose that cost?" I said: "I wonder how many people got killed building that thing?" We all responded from our basic mind-set. Our presuppositions about what mattered most guided our interpretation. Our faith shaped our understanding.

Berkouwer has used a suggestive definition for a scientific Christian theology rooted in the Augustinian tradition. I found this sentence in a speech he once gave to first-year seminary students: "Theology is scientific reflection on the normativity of revelation for faith."

The scientific theologian and the simple believer both begin from a personal faith commitment to God revealed in Jesus Christ. They both accept revelation as normative for them. That is, they treat the Biblical data as having ultimate value and valid application to their lives. And they both reflect, they think about God. The professional theologian is distinguished from any other believer only in that the theologian has the training and tools for doing "scientific" reflection. The theologian is equipped with specialized knowledge of the nature of the Biblical material and its relation to other data and with specialized tools for understanding the intricacies of the data being studied. The theologian is just one specialist serving the body of Christ. He or she provides specialized analysis which the community can then put to practical use. A Christian scientific theologian must combine specialized competence and self-conscious commitment to the presuppositions of the Christian faith.

Christianity in All of Life

Presuppositions govern not just theology but all of life. Dutch Christians have recognized this and applied it with a vengeance. In Holland, your religious faith determines your whole way of life. The newspaper you pick up in the morning is a Protestant, a Roman Catholic, a Socialist, or a Communist newspaper. The radio station you tune in, the television channel you select, bring in Protestant, Roman Catholic, Socialist, or humanist networks and programs. There are Protestant labor unions and management groups and Protestant political parties. All have their Roman Catholic, Socialist, and Communist counterparts. And rather than piously saying that individual Christians should be involved in society, they have formed Christian organizations that make a difference.

A man named Abraham Kuyper sparked the reorganization of his whole country. Kuyper lived in the nineteenth century. He was educated in the extreme liberal tradition and took his doctorate in theology at Leiden. While in the pastorate, he sensed the inadequacy of his liberal presuppositions. Somehow he worked his way back to a historical, Augustinian orthodoxy. Then he went to work! Before he was done he had founded a denomination and a university, edited a leading daily newspaper, and organized a political party. Eventually he became prime minister of the Netherlands. That is applying Christianity to all of life!

One of Kuyper's central principles was "sphere sovereignty." He felt that there were three basic "spheres" or centers of influence. They were: the home, the church, and the state. He was always asking: In whose sphere of influence does this problem belong? For example, who has the responsibility for educating children? Kuyper's answer: The state is responsible to see that children *are* educated, but the family is responsible to decide *how* its children are educated. So he developed Christian schools. They were not parochial schools, run by the church. Christian schools are private schools, run by associations of Christian parents. In addition to Protestant schools there are Roman Catholic schools and so-called neutral (or humanist) schools. And the state pays for them all! All three spheres work together. I am not suggesting that we can just pick up this method and transplant it to the United States. Our culture imposes its own peculiar problems. Some of the Protestant and Roman Catholic schools in this country have been used by parents to flee from real life. Private schools that allow themselves to be used—e.g., as an escape from racial integration—are hardly worthy expressions of our piety. What counts is that we face our presuppositions. What matters even more is that we try to begin from Christian presuppositions.

The Subject of Theology

Every science is distinguished not only by its faith—its presuppositions—but by its subject matter. The body of data that theology studies is revelation—the gospel, the Biblical witness to Christ and his salvation, with its multiple implications. That is the subject of our theological investigation. The method we use must take into account the unique character of our subject. The Biblical writers are witnessing to their experience of a person. They are not primarily outlining a system of abstract ideas. The object of theology therefore is not a fixed, static object that we can manipulate, but a living, dynamic person.

T. F. Torrance of Edinburgh has written extensively on theology as a science. He claims that the radical difference between theological science and other sciences lies in the object of our study. This "object" is really a living subject—"God himself in his speaking and acting." God revealed in Jesus Christ can never be the mere object of our inquiries. He is a subject who lays claim on us and asks for our commitment to himself.

What is the practical value of seeing theology as a science? It is to remind us that there is a difference between what God says and what we say about him. The curse of much systematic theology has been the implicit identification of the theologian's propositional statements with God's words. We interpret God's Word. We do it prayerfully, and we try to do it skillfully.

But we do it. And our interpretations are not divine. They are scientific. That is, they are experimental. They are the best we can do now. As we mature in the Christian faith we will do better. We learn, as in all science, by trial and error.

The Procedures of Science

A scientist builds models of reality. A model is not the same as the real thing. But it helps us to understand reality. A model takes the essential pieces of the real thing and scales them down so that we can understand them. That is to say, we speak of God by analogies, models from life. We say God is our Father. We mean that we see in his acts some of the best characteristics of certain fathers we know. When we forget that we are making models and speaking by analogies we run the risk of idolatry. Idolatry consists in worshiping the created model rather than pointing to the creator it represents. We must not get too attached to our thought forms, our fine distinctions of language, our cultural packaging.

Genuine scientists are profoundly humble. The great thinkers know how little they really know. Theological science too is a human and fallible enterprise. We can learn from our mistakes. Mistakes can be expected and can be forgiven. At least they *should* be, especially in Christian scientific work. Some people are offended by the critical dimension in theological work. Herman Bavinck, who followed Abraham Kuyper as professor of dogmatics at the Free University of Amsterdam, had a helpful answer to that. He asserted that the only kind of criticism which was really damaging to Christianity was criticism that came from the heart. He admitted that personal resistance to God can dwell quite as comfortably in dead orthodoxy as it can in the most extreme liberalism. It was Bavinck who reminded us that we are always in danger of having faith in our confession rather than confessing our faith.

In America we often do theology as if it was a game of cops and robbers. We choose up sides, thinking that the "good guys" (those we agree with) say and do all good things and that the "bad guys" (those we disagree with) say and do all bad things. Life isn't like that. I can remember how puzzled I was when I started reading G. C. Berkouwer to discover his quoting Rudolf Bultmann, for instance, with great approval in one place and then a few pages later vigorously disagreeing with him. He didn't seem to need to add a footnote to remind us that Bultmann was a bad guy. He dealt with the issues instead of putting down the people. Scientific theology enables us to learn from anyone engaged in the same science. It also gives us a chance to disagree with someone's theology without questioning his or her morality or personal Christian faith. Theology is not faith. Faith is a trustful commitment of the whole person to Christ. Theology is our careful, orderly thought about the revelation in Scripture of the God in whom we have faith. Theology and faith go together. You really can't have one without the other. But each has its distinctive role. Faith is primary. Theology is the necessary next step.

Theology for the Laity

When theology is called a science some might fear that this makes Biblical interpretation the property of a scientifically trained elite. Not so in Holland. There, theology professors train pastors who train people to be good theologians. I was amazed by the theological understanding of our Dutch Christian friends. How did they get that way? Take a look at the pattern of life of a typical Dutch Christian family. It begins, let's say, at marriage. The minister always presents the couple with a Bible and admonishes them to read it as a family. And they do read it at table, after the evening meal each day.

In America our young people join the church around the age of twelve to fourteen. I guess that is because we think they are psychologically ready then. A Dutch young person at twelve is just ready to begin catechism. Students meet with the minister once a week after school in a small class. They study Scripture and its historical interpretation in the creeds and catechisms of their church. This goes on for about *six years.* No Dutch Christian would think of joining the church before the age of eighteen or twenty. I asked some friends of ours why they waited so long. Their reply was: "How could you possibly know enough unless you had that much training?" You may feel sorry for those poor kids going to catechism class all those years. I feel sorry for the minister! He has used all his standard stuff with them. That really puts the pressure on him to come up with something deeper on Sunday morning. Dutch sermons are full of solid Biblical and theological content because the people want it. And they can take it.

I remember one Sunday after church being invited to the home of a Dutch friend. She was a retired school teacher. Sharee and I and another couple sat in the autumn sunshine on her tiny back porch. She looked around with a smile of contentment and said: "This is the loveliest hour of the week. We have been to worship. We are together. A good cup of coffee. And now—to attack the sermon!" And wrestle with it she did, and we did, together. When American Christians spend Sunday dinner discussing the points of the preacher instead of the place of their pro team we'll know we are making progress. Training in scientific theology can give us tools for evangelical practice.

Lay people need not fear scientific theology. In the first place we are all theologians. We all think about God. That's all *theos* ("God") and *logos* ("word," "thought") mean. So we might as well think together, learning from each other. Secondly, we should keep clear the distinction between two levels of approach to the Bible. The first level is the central, saving message of the gospel. That level is open to all who can read or will listen to the simple story of God's good creation, man's sinful fall and Christ's gracious life, death, and resurrection for our salvation. The approach to that simple, central message is through faith.

Around that saving center lies a vast body of supporting material that is often complex, difficult to interpret, and subject to a variety of understandings. Didn't Peter complain that "our beloved brother Paul" often said things which were difficult to interpret (II Peter 3:15–16)? The insistence of individuals and groups on their own private interpretations in this complex area has led to untold dispute, disharmony, and division within the Christian community. The approach to this level is through science. This is where a theologian is needed and can be useful. A theologian's task is to serve the church by making available historical, cultural, and philosophical background and concepts. With these we can better understand the meaning of the Biblical message in the culture to which it came. Then we can translate that message into sensible and usable models adapted to our present culture. Always we need to recognize that our models are human approximations and not divine interpretations. We need to listen to the expert's wisdom and one another's experience when we struggle with the difficult passages.

At the very practical level you have no doubt been involved, as I have, in many useless arguments. Often they root in a failure to distinguish between the central message of Scripture and the nature of its supporting material. I can remember a woman questioning me once in a Sunday school class. She insisted that we should prove that there could have been a fish big enough to swallow Jonah. I submit to you that this is not a question of the saving message of Scripture. Nor does it help us understand the particular message of the book of Jonah. It is a scientific question best settled by consulting Biblical experts on the literary genre, the cultural expectations, and the historical setting of that book. But notice how this question diverts attention from the real message of the prophet. How many people who are worked up over the big fish know what the book of Jonah is about? Do they know that this book tells about a prejudiced preacher who refused to preach the gospel to people racially and nationally different from him? How our prejudice thwarts God's evangelism is very close to the heart of the Biblical message. Thank God, the book of Jonah testifies that God is gracious in spite of us. He will keep after us even when we resist him. Scientific theology is no cure for our resistance to the Holy Spirit. It can help clear up honest misunderstandings. Best of all, it continually points us to the heart of Scripture —Christ and his salvation—and helps us to avoid becoming entangled on the periphery. That kind of science conserves the gospel message but not all our old, uncritical ideas. That kind of theology is evangelical in freeing our faith to concentrate on the main issues.

CHAPTER 5

The Communion
of Saints

After our first year in Amsterdam we were almost out of money. For months we cast about for some source of funds to enable us to stay in Holland so that I could continue to study. At the last moment a quite unexpected opportunity appeared. My wife, Sharee, who has an M.S. in Speech Pathology, had gone to the large International School in The Hague in hopes of persuading them that they needed a speech therapist. Instead, the headmaster persuaded her that she was needed to teach fifth and sixth grades in a new branch of the school. An American corporation had dropped about forty American families in a smaller city in the south of Holland named Dordrecht. These Americans were to start a plant to manufacture their company's product. The city had no facilities for foreigners, and so by arrangement with the International School there were to be three classrooms for English-speaking children in a local Dutch public ("neutral") school. My wife became the teacher in one of those classrooms.

Starting from Scratch

On the day we arrived, an American engineer, who was the liaison between the plant and the school, met us. One of his first comments to me was: "And what do you do?" I replied that I was a Presbyterian minister doing graduate work in the Netherlands. Immediately he exclaimed: "We need you too!" He explained that many of the Americans, representing the lay leadership of many different congregations in the United States, had already been seeking a means of having church services in English. Now, providentially, here was an American minister appearing in their midst. At first I resisted. "I have a full-time job with my studies," I protested. But—I believe that God calls a person to a particular field of ministry. Here was a congregation seeking the ministry of the Word. I was the only minister in the vicinity who could minister in their language to their particular needs. I became persuaded that this was a call. Thus began a life-changing two-year period. We learned by experience that the Bible was freshly understood when read in the fellowship of the church. This congregation represented more dimensions of the church than we had previously known. It was truly a communion of the saints.

How do you form a congregation with representatives of seven or eight American denominations in the midst of a foreign country with no precedents or rule books to follow? This first wave of Americans had been well oriented by their company and knew they were not to form a separate American ghetto. They applied the same principles to the church. Instead of forming a separate American congregation, we approached the largest of the Dutch Reformed denominations in the city (Nederlandse Hervormde Kerk) and asked if we might somehow become guest members of one of their churches. The effect on them was overwhelming. They had expected the Americans to be snobbish. Their response overwhelmed us. They gave us the use of their newest church building. They even changed the hour of the regular morning service to a half hour *earlier* to accommodate our worship service! In time, I was officially installed as a minister of the Dutch Reformed Church by action of their General Synod and my Presbytery. We had freedom to work out our own problems. But we had the backing and support of the larger church in that place, which gave us encouragement and a sense of responsibility.

What kind of worship service do you have to meet the needs of such a diverse group of Christians? In our congregation we had Episcopalians and Southern Baptists, Northern and Southern Presbyterians, Lutherans and Methodists, Dutch visitors, English-speaking persons of other nationalities, and many others. So, we elected a worship committee composed of representatives from each distinct group among us. Then the committee met in someone's living room a number of times until we came to a simple order of worship that was satisfactory to all. I volunteered to preach on Biblical themes summarized in the Apostles' Creed, since that was a doctrinal standard familiar and common to us all. But what about the sacraments? The group wanted the Lord's Supper once a month. But in what form were we to have it? We all were used to partaking in different ways: some coming forward to kneel, others having the elements served in the pew, some with individual servings and others with a common loaf and cup. To our great surprise we discovered that our host church, the Dutch Reformed, had found meaningful a different service than any of us had experienced. We adopted it. In the Dutch Reformed Church there is a communion table at the front of the sanctuary that is a real, not just a symbolic, table. Thirty-three people at a time could come forward and sit together around that table. I stood and passed a common loaf while together we raised our individual cups. There we were, really sitting together at the Lord's table, representing many different theological traditions, different languages, cultures, and races. I was always moved. It was a genuine communion of saints!

Sacrament and Salvation

Our congregation named itself "The Pilgrim Fellowship." We were English-speaking people seeking religious freedom and growth in a strange land just as some of our antecedents had come from England to America by way of Holland in an earlier pilgrimage. The members of our congregation were mostly of early middle age. I performed no weddings or funerals, but there were numerous infant baptisms. The first request to baptize an infant came from a binational couple. The mother was of Dutch parentage, had grown up in Argentina, and belonged to the Scottish Presbyterian Church. The husband was a prominent Dutch attorney from an antichurch family. They had become adherents of our congregation, since they could not feel at home in the Dutch churches. I had not yet been officially installed, so a Dutch Reformed minister assisted me in performing the actual sacrament. My Dutch colleague had been influenced by the modest liturgical revival going on in his denomination. He had become convinced that the proper mode of baptism was neither immersion nor sprinkling, but *pouring!* Accordingly, when the day came, the trembling mother held her baby out at arm's length while our Dutch Dominie poured three great handfuls of water over the baby's head: "in the name of the Father, and the Son, and the Holy

Ghost." The chancel was awash! They all got safely back to their seats with no accidents and I breathed a sigh of relief. At the door I shook hands with the people as they departed and I remember vividly the greeting from one Southern gentlewoman: "I just want to thank you for the lovely service, especially the drowning of the baby!"

About a year later that baby's father, Martin, came to me and requested baptism. This man had grown up very much aware that the churches generally represented certain classes of people, and stood for certain cultural and political ideologies which he could not share. The cultural encasement of the church had prevented him from hearing the gospel. (This is the other, the problem side of Kuyper's cultural reformation.) For this Dutch lawyer, the Pilgrim Fellowship was different. Here were people from different cultures and diverse political ideologies who seemed bound together simply by their need for each other and their common allegiance to Christ. This congregation, by its own request, had almost none of the usual organizations. But the members requested a study course on "What Christians Believe," and 50 percent of the congregation turned out each Wednesday night for seven weeks. In this setting, our Dutch friend could hear the gospel. He professed his faith in Christ and was baptized.

One, Holy, Catholic Church

This Dutch attorney's experience causes me to reflect on the nature of the church. The creeds speak of "one, holy, catholic church." We believe that in heaven we will be one with all other Christians. There Christ's high-priestly prayer will be fulfilled. But we often fail to note the reason for which Christ prayed that his disciples might be one. Our Lord prayed "that the world may *believe* . . . that the world may *know* that thou hast sent me" (John 17:21,23). For Jesus Christ the evident, visible unity of his followers was a means of evangelism! In the Pilgrim Fellowship we were one. We had to be. All the competing traditions and all the familiar customs were absent. We knew we needed each other and that our unity in Christ was far more important than anything that divided us. That visible, workable unity was evangelical. It was a means of proclaiming the good news that Christ redeems and changes lives. That living witness supported and interpreted the verbal witness in a decisive way. The church is one.

The church is also to be holy. That means "set apart." It means that the church is not to conform to the world's standards. Yet think of the church in the United States. What does the traditional church look like? Recent Gallup Poll statistics give an objective outline of the way we must look to nonbelievers. Over 40 percent of adult church members in the United States attend church in a typical week. That is better than in most other countries in the world. However, other statistics make clear that there is a direct correlation between the economic, social, and educational position of a person and the church to which that person belongs. We all know quite well which Protestant church in a moderate-sized city is likely to have in its membership the economic, social, and educational elite. In most cities it would be the Episcopal church. We Presbyterians are still climbing that ladder of worldly success. We are only second, but we try harder! Third would be the Lutherans, followed by the Methodists and the Baptists, to mention only these five large groupings. You also know that you can read that scale politically. The higher you get on the social ladder, the more likely you are traditionally to be a Republican. The closer you come to the Baptists, the nearer you are to the

Democrats. But much more important than the above profile is the fact that statistically there is no difference between church members and non-church members in their attitudes toward moral and social issues. What church people belong to, or whether they even belong to a church, seems to make no difference in their attitudes toward racism, or war, or pollution.

The picture of the traditional church as seen by non-Christians must be clear. The church can be classed as a private club. It seems to sanction the self-interest of its members. It defends the *status quo* of its members' particular subculture. That is why evangelical Christians must beware of rejoicing too simply in the fact that conservative churches are growing. Church growth *may* be the result of comfortable conformity to the secular culture. The most rigid set of doctrinal standards doesn't protect a congregation from giving its primary allegiance to Caesar when the chips are down. The Gallup Poll researchers asked Christians and non-Christians alike what they would do if a black family moved next door. Two thirds of both groups said that they would move. To give primary allegiance to the values of the local community is a form of idolatry. Baal was the god of the local, settled inhabitants. Praying primarily for the harvest and proclaiming business as usual was never recognized by the prophets as valid religion.

For the church to be truly evangelical it must be one, holy, and catholic (universal). For the good news to be heard it must be proclaimed by all kinds of people to all kinds of people. It cannot be just the private property of an "in" group who share it only with their own kind of folks. That is why identifying the word "evangelical" with a certain ecclesiastical or social subculture is a dangerous business. Being "evangelical" means bearing the good news! It means concentration on the gospel. There is no good news for the world if the gospel has attached to it a multitude of unspoken prior conditions—how you must look, how you should talk, and how you should live before you can believe. At the *least*, that is law, and not gospel. The law doesn't save, especially if it is the unwritten law of man's social self-justification.

If we are honest with ourselves, we can confess that our model of churchmanship is often the model of the Pharisees. The Pharisees were the good church people. They did everything according to the rules. They liked doing things the way they had always done them. Perhaps that is why Jesus did not choose his disciples from among the church people. He called a crooked tax collector named Matthew. He socialized with Matthew's friends—"many bad characters," according to Scripture (Mark 2:15, NEB). To the question of the scandalized Pharisees, "Why does he eat with tax collectors and sinners?" (Mark 2:16) Jesus' answer is simple. He went to people who knew they needed help, not to people who judged themselves good because of their conformity to their community.

I don't think I could have seen that in the gospel if I had not been reading the Scripture in the fellowship of the breadth of the church. I need the whole church catholic as my context to help me see what is my cultural bias and what is Christian belief. God is undoubtedly willing to begin with people where they are in whatever culture. As we communicate across cultural barriers we can perceive the gospel more clearly and evaluate what cultural changes the gospel demands.

Being "in" but not "of" the world is hard. In the summer of 1961 Sharee and I accompanied a group of American high school kids to a camp in the Taunus Mountains of Germany. They were from the Pilgrim Fellowship and from two other

American congregations in Europe. These kids were bright and healthy. Their parents were U.S. embassy and military people and business executives. We had lots of time to talk together. Each morning at the camp we had a Bible study. Then we broke up into small groups to discuss assigned questions. One morning the question was: "Are there values which can't be bought?" Now, to the mind of the college religion professor who was leading the study the answer seemed obvious. But the kids were honest enough to give the wrong answer! The world they lived in had taught them that everything can be bought. Popularity, status, security—they were all purchasable commodities. Not necessarily with money, you understand, but if you play your cards right and know the right people, you can get what you want. A second question was: "Do we try to buy God's love?" I remember one blond sixteen-year-old saying in real anguish, "If we can't buy it in some way, how can we get it?" The Biblical idea that God's love in Christ is a free gift is foreign to our society. These young people were honest enough to admit what we often think but suppress. We are conditioned by our culture. Our ideas are formed by the world around us: newspapers, magazines, movies, television, schools, and friends. H. G. Wells once said that the voice of our neighbors sounds louder in our ears than the voice of God. That isn't really very surprising considering the small amount of our time which God gets. The media do much better! It's easy and common to put Christian name tags on ingrained worldly attitudes. I was caught up short recently when the message of a Sunday sermon got through to me (it can happen!). The text was: "I can do all things in him who strengthens me" (Phil. 4:13). The context concerns being content with our circumstances. For years I have used that text to justify my impatient, aggressive competitiveness. Now I have lost my comfortable Christian cover for that worldly attitude. We need the communion of saints. We need the whole, holy, catholic church. We need the corrective of other Christians so that we can hear the gospel clearly. To listen to one another as we listen to the Word is evangelical.

CHAPTER 6

The Image of God in Humanity

Listening to young people has often improved my theology. While serving the Pilgrim Fellowship in Dordrecht, we took a busload of American high school young people on a weekend trip to visit their counterparts in the American community in Bad Godesberg, Germany. One of the weekend activities was a trip along the Rhine to visit Maria Lach, the oldest Roman Catholic monastery on the European continent.

The Monk of Maria Lach

Maria Lach is a center for liturgical studies and has a marvelous library that draws scholars from all over the world. When we arrived, we were met by an English-speaking German monk who was to lead us on a tour through the place. Apparently there were more of us than expected and the German monk was having great difficulty being heard by the whole group. Some of the young people on the edges of the group were beginning to drift off. I was wondering what to do. Just then, through a side door of the room in which we were standing, came another monk. He was dressed like all the others in a black cassock that reached from his throat to his ankles. But he was quite tall and very handsome. He looked very much like the American movie star Charlton Heston. With two tablets of stone he could have played Moses in *The Ten Commandments.* He turned out to be an American Trappist monk on leave from his order (and from his vow of silence) to study at Maria Lach. So we divided into two groups. One group followed the German monk, and the other, mostly the girls, followed "Charlton Heston." Fearing a Pied Piper episode, I went with the girls and their handsome American guide.

There are few more interesting experiences than watching the interaction between romantic high school girls and a handsome monk. The girls asked questions unrelated to Maria Lach, such as "Have you ever been in love?" And the monk had a good time teasing them in return. Finally someone asked the really crucial question: "What does a monk do?" Our affable guide suddenly became irritated. He replied: "You don't understand at all. I don't *do* anything! Oh, I milk a cow once in a while. I study in the library. And I pray at Mass. But none of those have anything to do with my being a monk. As a monk, I don't *do* anything. I *think!* I glorify God just by thinking about him."

Further talk with that monk and subsequent study have helped me to understand the logic of his position. Thomas Aquinas, the systematizer of medieval Catholicism, built his theology on a synthesis of the philosophy of Aristotle and the witness of Scripture. All that we needed to know about nature and natural law, Aristotle had already told us. What we needed to know about the supernatural and the grace of God, we learned from the Bible. It was Aristotle who taught us that "Man is a rational animal." Furthermore, in his ethical writings Aristotle proclaimed that man was good insofar as he fulfilled his highest capacity. If man's highest distinctive capacity is reason, then to flee from the world, to avoid active involvement, simply to *think*, is indeed the highest good and would be to the glory of God.

When I began to teach in a church-related liberal arts college I met the spirit of that monk again. This time it was in a textbook on basic Christian doctrines written by conservative evangelicals. The essay on the doctrine of the image of God in man outlined a traditional view that I had long taken for granted. The basic thrust of this view is that the image of God in humans resides in certain "spiritual qualities" that are like qualities in God himself. Can you guess what these qualities are? *Knowledge* is the first and foremost. Then come *righteousness* and *holiness.* More importantly, these qualities are usually grouped into two categories: the image in the broader sense—rational (knowledge); and the image in the narrower sense—moral (righteousness and holiness). Why is that important? Because, according to this view, when Adam fell into sin the image in the broader (rational) sense was not damaged. Notice our monk's Aristotelian assumption that what makes humans distinct from other creatures is that they think! Sin destroyed the image of God in the narrower (moral) sense. The implication is clear. Sin resides primarily in the moral, emotional, even physical aspects of human beings. The head is O.K. The body is bad.

When I began to teach that view I realized that I didn't believe it anymore. It divided man into two separate compartments—head and heart, mind and body. It contradicted what I knew of psychology. Furthermore, it denied the basic Biblical emphasis on man as a whole person. In the accounts of humanity's creation in Gen., chs. 1 and 2, there is no indication of such compartmentalization. Nor is there any indication that somehow the mind is superior to the body. "The Lord God formed man of dust from the ground, and breathed into his nostrils the breath of life; and man became a living being"—a total, integrated personality (Gen. 2:7)!

It seemed further that this dualistic view of humankind was founded on a dubious method of using Scripture. Three words are plucked from two verses referring to "image" in the New Testament, without regard to their larger context. "Knowledge" comes from Col. 3:10, "righteousness" and "holiness" come from Eph. 4:24. These three words are then used as the symbols of an extensive and systematic view of humanity that contains many assumptions that are present neither in the words themselves nor in the context of their use. Words that Paul used as illustrations in a practical, pastoral context are lifted out and used as definitions in a philosophical, theoretical context.

The central *truth* of Scripture is not contained in any theoretical statement, but is revealed in a person, Jesus Christ. Our Lord said: "I am the way, and the *truth*, and the life" (John 14:6). The Greek word for "truth," *alētheia*, implies the unveiling of what is hidden. It points to an idea that is clear and evident. The Hebrew word for "truth" is related to the verb *aman* (cf. "amen"). The Hebrew concept of truth points to a person who is steadfast and faithful. The Bible is not interested in knowledge for knowledge's sake. The Bible calls "truth" that which leads to righteous life.

Jesus' statement that *he is* the *truth* is asserted in the context of Thomas' desire for knowledge. Jesus asks Thomas to trust in him, not first of all to discover more about him (John 14:5–6). The Spirit is called the "Spirit of truth." In the same context the Spirit is called the "Counselor" (John 14:16,17). The Spirit will grant us truth at the functional, experiential level as He witnesses to Christ. The Spirit does not intend nor grant theoretical certainty. The history of disagreement over truth in the church makes that evident. Keeping Christ's commandments isn't related to having a certain method of interpretation or a perfect system of understanding. Our ability to keep Christ's commandments is related to how well we love him (John 14:15). Jesus' disciples operated just as we do. They continually wanted certain knowledge. Jesus instead called them and calls us to trustful obedience. A classic case is recorded in Acts, ch. 1. The disciples are with their Lord for the last time prior to his ascension into heaven. At such a crucial moment, what do the disciples want? One last bit of inside information—"Lord, will you at this time restore the kingdom to Israel?" Jesus' last words are a reminder that such knowledge is none of their business. Power will come from the Holy Spirit. Their task is to be "witnesses" to their relationship with the living Christ (Acts 1:6–8).

Reaffirming relationship is crucial to rightly understanding theological statements. German theologian Helmut Thielicke has most helpfully pointed out that theology is only properly done as dialogue with God. Our purpose is not a final statement of "objective" truth. The purpose of theology is rather to listen to what God says and to become involved in making a personal reply. Sin came into human experience the first time that God was spoken of in the (objective) third person instead of the (relational) second person. The serpent spoke not *to* God but *about* him. Remember the sneering question, "Did God say, 'You shall not eat of any tree of the garden'?" (Gen. 3:1.) The question was stated objectively. But the context was so distorted that the person, forgetting the relationship, could turn away from God.

Christian theology originated when Christ asked his disciples, "Who do you say that I am?" Peter replied, "You are the

Christ, the Son of the living God" (Matt. 16:16). That is the first doctrinal statement uttered in the form of a confession. Peter's confessional statement witnesses to his personal relationship with Christ. We need to state what we believe with as much clarity as we can. But the particular formulation of any doctrinal statement should never become an end in itself. We need to try to organize our beliefs into a sensible, useful whole. But we must resist the temptation to twist and tug the Biblical data into forms that suit our systematic theology.

We do need a viewpoint that gives meaning to life. A national study made by the American Council on Education revealed that 86 percent of college freshmen considered it essential to develop a philosophy of life. That was more important to students than anything else. My experience in teaching college students is that they don't want all the answers—an airtight system. They want what Søren Kierkegaard wanted as a Danish student a century ago. "Confronted with the Hegelian system [which had all the answers] at the University of Copenhagen, he reacted strongly against it. It could not supply what he needed—'a truth which is true *for me,* to find *the idea for which I can live and die.*' " It is for Christ, and him only, that we should be willing to live and die (Phil. 1:21). Our commitment to him as the truth must always be qualitatively different from our attachment to the truths we state about him.

Scripture never promises salvation through theoretical knowledge. We receive Christ through trusting faith. We should not expect to grow with him in any other way. Our faith gives us a framework on which to hang the facts that come to us. We must never let that framework of thought become a theoretical structure divorced from our personal relationship to Christ. Calvin began his *Institutes* with the affirmation: "Nearly all the wisdom we possess, that is to say, true and sound wisdom, consists of two parts: the knowledge of God and of ourselves." That kind of knowledge is relational knowledge. It is perhaps best expressed in relational terms. Today the language of the social sciences—especially psychology, sociology, and anthropology—offers more useful forms for our theological statements than Aristotelian philosophy does.

Athens and Jerusalem

Christians have always struggled with the relationship between Athens and Jerusalem. The names of these two cities have symbolized the difference between philosophy and theology, between reason and relationship. A Latin theologian in the third century took the one extreme. "What has Athens to do with Jerusalem?" Tertullian demanded: "What concord is there between the Academy and the Church?" He still offers proof texts for Christian anti-intellectuals, though he was an intellectual and a philosopher himself. He said of the crucifixion of the Son of God: "It is by all means to be believed because it is absurd." On the other extreme were the early Greek theologians, such as Origen and Clement. They felt that the best of Greek philosophy was inspired by the *Logos*, or Word of God, who was incarnate in Christ. In their view a knowledge of Greek philosophy was meant to be the entrance to Christianity for Greeks. They did not hesitate to assert that the classic Greek philosophers were Christians.

Where are we in this conflict? Somewhere in the middle. Our philosophy, our way of thinking, is something we learn. It is part of our culture. It is not divine. We in the Western world have learned our way of thinking from the Greeks. That is our culture. We begin in Athens. We value the rational, the analytic, and the systematic—so much so that great movements such as existentialism have swung completely the other way in reaction. Very few of us live in the world of the existentialist, however. Mostly we live in the world of the machine, of conformity to the dictates of society, of obedience to the stimuli of Madison Avenue. Our culture is an increasingly technological one that dehumanizes persons. It subordinates human values to material values. It seeks to control our persons and our destinies by fixing us within a technological frame of reference. We need to journey to Jerusalem. We need the Hebraic personal touch. It would do us good to have prophetic passion, corporate commitment, Israelite imagination. We need to be new persons relating in new ways to our culture. After we have been to Jerusalem, then we can come back to our technological Athens. We can accept its discipline, testing, and sharpening. We can face its challenges and problems and frustrations. We can do this because our faith is rooted in a personal relationship to Christ. Our faith is not based on the thought forms acquired in our culture, though it is expressed through them. Neither the questions we are asked nor the answers we give ultimately determine our salvation. What matters is whose person we are.

What makes a person human is not reason, but relationship. We aren't thinking animals. We are worshiping animals. Only humans will sacrifice everything for God or an idol. God holds all persons in relationship to himself. But that relationship, like human relations, can be one of harmony or one of tension. When persons are obedient to God they increasingly reflect as a mirror the character of the One with whom they are in loving fellowship. Sin is turning our back to God, presenting the dark and tarnished side of the mirror. What people's sins reflect are the fruits of a relationship gone wrong. They show the signs of antagonism and strained personal bonds. It is not rationality that keeps human beings human. It is the fact that God in his common grace keeps all persons in a relationship to himself. He restrains even the most rebellious of his children from the dehumanizing consequences of their sin.

There was one person who fully reflected the image of God. Jesus Christ *is* "the image of the invisible God" (Col. 1:15). He lived and grew in a fully harmonious relationship to his heavenly Father. It is when we identify ourselves fully with Jesus Christ, when we commit ourselves to union with him, that we begin to grow in the image of the invisible God. Growth in Christian maturity, what theologians have called "sanctification," is the reflection in our lives of a growing relationship with our Creator and Lord.

When we turn to the Bible we discover the story of human beings' relationship to God. This story is told in relational terms. It is not a recital of God's ideas given just to our minds. It is the warm, reassuring story of God, who like a Father cares for the whole of us in our whole life situation. The Bible is replete with stories of real people rebelling and being reconciled to the real God. We should not impose on Scripture a demand that it produce rational (in our terms) rules, and objective, impersonal truths. We can be grateful that it provides deep insights into God's relationships with persons—expressed in personal terms to which we can personally relate. Recognition of the personal, relational dimension of Scripture is for me a mark of an increasingly evangelical understanding of Scripture.

Chapter 7

Childbirth
and Bible Translation

We had been married five years. Now we were expecting our first child. Sharee had taught American children in Dordrecht for two years. I had served during the same two years as pastor of the Pilgrim Fellowship. We both resigned from our jobs and began the push toward finishing my graduate work. We hoped that the money we had saved from our two Dutch salaries would see us through.

Natural Childbirth

In Holland, having a baby is a family affair. The father is expected to be present not only at conception but at birth. Having a baby is a normal, healthy activity. You can't even get health insurance coverage for pregnancy. An expectant mother isn't sick. Babies are delivered without giving the mother a general anesthetic. After all, she is in charge and knows what to do.

We had never had a baby before. As a speech therapist in the United States, Sharee had taken many case histories of handicapped children. Stories from the mothers of those children had given her an impression of childbirth as involving tremendous pain, isolation, and betrayal. During the first year of our marriage even the idea of pregnancy was abhorrent. We struggled with these feelings as a couple. We searched the Scriptures for help. Yes, women shall have pain in childbirth. The Old Testament, the New Testament, and Christian friends confirmed this bleak outlook. What an ironic contrast —begun in love, delivered in despair! Where was God's grace in it all?

Children enjoy a high priority in Dutch culture. A New Testament professor at the Free University was president of the "Rich Nest" society. You had to have at least five children to qualify for membership. Large families were greatly approved. Sharee wondered, is it masochism, or fulfillment? Prenatal and well-baby clinics are provided. And childbirth preparation classes are also common. So Sharee began attending classes for expectant mothers. She learned how her body would function and what to do during delivery. She did exercises to prepare. Besides, like other Dutch housewives she walked to the shops, did her washing by hand, and daily rode her bicycle. Finally we were able to discuss what she was learning in class and begin to focus on what would happen. I was groping to understand my role. We began to get the message from Dutch culture that childbirth is an event to rehearse and share, not a horrifying surprise, to be forgotten as soon as possible. One of the American women in the Pilgrim Fellowship was especially supportive. She had had natural childbirth in the United States and lent Sharee her copy of Grantly Dick-Read's *Childbirth Without Fear.*

Finally the day came. It was Saturday evening. We were visiting with American student friends. We had just had dinner and were listening to language records, trying to learn French. The contractions started to come regularly. We went home and called a cab to take us to the hospital. In Holland most children are born at home, with the assistance of a midwife. That was too much for our American upbringing. We were two steps farther up the ladder. We were going to a hospital. And we had a medical doctor who was an obstetrician.

The doctor was in the hospital minutes after we arrived. Upon examination, he assured us that "It has begun!" The baby wouldn't be born until morning. He suggested that I could go home for the night if I wished. Like a fool, I did. I was miserable. What could I do? I spent a lot of time praying frantically. Finally I fell into fitful sleep for a few hours. (I didn't know until later what a horrible place the "fathers' waiting room" is at most hospitals. But I knew then that I didn't ever again want to spend time away from Sharee at such an important moment.) At 6:00 A.M. the nurse, who came to do some needlework while she waited with my wife, called to say that my wife would welcome me back. Sharee was fine. The nurse had just brought her tea and rusk and offered me breakfast. I gladly accepted. I wasn't so glad when it turned out to be two cold liver sandwiches—nourishing, normal, but not my usual bacon and eggs!

We ate in the delivery room that Sunday morning. I wasn't scrubbed, gowned, or anything. I was in my street clothes. But I was there, sitting beside Sharee. We were holding hands. I'm sure it did me as much good as it did her. Two nurses were close by, completing morning duties, asking, "Are you having contractions?" I read to Sharee, "Come to me, all who labor and are heavy laden, and I will give you rest" (Matt. 11:28). That gave comfort. But did we really understand what labor was? Just prior to the second stage, the doctor was called. True to the nurse's prediction, he was there in five minutes. When the doctor advised Sharee to push she would push. Then we would wait and relax. The labor got harder. Perspiration stood on her forehead as she worked. Then, there was the baby! I was the first one to yell: "It's a boy!" He was wet and blue and beautiful. And Sharee was in ecstasy. I had never seen her so happy as when they laid that wet, naked baby in her arms. It was the most exciting moment of our married lives. We were the most together. It was like an enormous sexual climax. Indeed it was. And it was meant to be. All of the waiting and work had been worth it. The next day Sharee reported that the hospital radio had been playing Handel's *Messiah*. She heard again, "His yoke is easy, and his burden is light." Now that made sense and we rejoiced.

Travel Trauma

A few months after Matthew's birth I finished my doctoral comprehensives. We were running out of money and I was running out of steam. We had been in Holland four years. Fortunately, I had been offered a job teaching at a Presbyterian liberal arts college. The letter making a definite offer came the day we brought Matthew home from the hospital. So in June of 1963 we returned to the United States.

It was a ghastly trip. We sailed from Rotterdam on a Norwegian freighter. Many people had told us that freighter travel was *the* way to go. And this was reputed to be a good line. But the captain of this particular ship hated passengers—and people in general. There were eleven passengers. We ate each meal at the captain's table in stony silence. If anyone commented, the captain would insult them. None of the mates ever came to meals. One of them was locked in his cabin, drunk. The others avoided the captain. Three days out to sea the milk all soured. Sharee was nursing Matthew, so that didn't leave us without food for our child. But each night the clock was turned back one half hour. That did affect us—terribly. A seven-month-old baby doesn't have a wristwatch to adjust. His stomach told him when to wake up, and that was at increasingly odd hours for us.

By the time we got to New York we were all worn out and psychologically confused. Then came the long trip across the country by car. Our house wasn't ready in Pennsylvania. So we boarded for two months, first with Sharee's parents and then with mine. The first thing everyone seemed to say to us on our return was: "You haven't changed at all." The motive was good. They wanted us to feel at home. But it wasn't true. Of course we had changed. After four years in Holland we were at home there. Coming back into our own culture was more difficult than adjusting to a foreign land. As foreigners in Holland we knew, and everyone else knew, that we had to change and adapt. When we returned to our own country it took even more changing and adapting. But we didn't recognize it as clearly. And others didn't realize what our needs were.

Parental Roles

In the midst of all the other changes, we were trying to learn to be parents. Marriage and parenthood are probably the most demanding and worthwhile tasks that human beings undertake. What very little training we get for these roles is inadequate and indirect. We had many conflicts over child-rearing. They rooted first of all in our differing personalities. Sharee is a second child. She is spontaneous, emotional, intuitive. And to top it off she is a "morning person." I am a first child. I'm methodical, controlled, analytical. And I'm a "night person." These differences caused real problems.

Our problems were compounded because I was very determined to be the "head of the house." And my ego was very damaged if I thought my authority was being questioned. Because I was a man, I thought I should have final authority. Intellectually, Sharee conceded. We both felt that as Christians that was right. But in practice it didn't always work. Especially it didn't work in raising children. It took me years to realize that Sharee's style of relating to the kids really was better. Abstract moral lectures are usually not as effective as hugs. A child is simply not an adult. Sharee understood child development and I didn't. I was big on principles. She understood little persons.

Fortunately, there was another Mister Rogers who came to our house regularly. Fred Rogers, of *Mister Rogers' Neighborhood* on educational television, is a Presbyterian minister who attended seminary about the same time I did. We've never met in person. But he is a welcome guest in our home via the television set. By listening to Sharee and watching the other Mister Rogers, I began to appreciate a different way of approaching children. And I came to understand that it was Christian as well as psychologically sound. Mister Rogers never uses religious language on his show. It is a good reminder that doing the truth is what is effective, rather than using a certain lingo. I'm still learning with Sharee and from others a more Biblical approach to family life, one which doesn't just copy patriarchal Hebrew and Greek culture.

Translation Problems

In the fall of 1963 we settled into college housing on a lovely curved street near a lake. All our neighbors were new junior faculty of about the same age as ourselves. As we got to know people and compared experiences, an unexpected pattern appeared. Sharee found that most of the American wives who had children were incredulous at her story of Matthew's birth. The typical reaction was so negative and disbelieving that she quit telling people about it. American women tended to view childbirth with fear and distaste. Despite all the technology of medical science and despite the anesthetics they had received, they described childbirth as a painful experience. Their husbands were mostly embarrassed and didn't want to discuss it. They felt somewhat guilty. But they hadn't been there and couldn't do anything about it. These Christians tended to feel that the Bible reinforced the unpleasant reality of their experience.

Sharee began to restudy Scripture to find all the citations having to do with childbirth. She sought insights from other women and shared her own. Then a friend introduced us to Helen Wessel's wonderful book, *Natural Childbirth and the Christian Family* (Harper & Row, 1963). Here was a couple whose struggles had been like our own. Helen Wessel was a mother. Her husband was a professor of Biblical language. Together they dealt with childbirth as a natural process of profound spiritual significance. They had grappled with mistranslations of the Hebrew and Greek that have fostered a mistaken acceptance of the necessity for pain in childbirth. We were learning an important lesson. We could trust our own experience. Sharee had not experienced "pain" in childbirth. Bringing her genuine experience to the Bible had helped us to understand the gospel message where the cultural bias of translators had obscured it.

After teaching for two years, we packed up again and headed back to finish my dissertation. Sharee had contacted ten hospitals in our area about our concern for sharing the experience of natural childbirth together. None would assure us that we would have a part in determining the procedure. We were quite willing therefore to have another child while we were overseas. Near the end of our year-and-a-half stay abroad we were back in Dordrecht. We were expecting our second child and wanted the same deeply significant experience of delivery. But the baby was not due until February, and I had to be back in the United States and teaching by the end of January. As we finished my graduation preparations, childbirth was much on our minds.

Part of a Dutch doctoral graduation is the presentation of some twenty *stellingen* ("theses"—like Martin Luther's Ninety-five Theses) that you are willing to defend, along with your printed dissertation, in public debate. My seventh *stelling* read: "In Genesis 3:16 'toil' is to be preferred to 'pain' as a translation of *'iṣṣābōn.*" Friends who were graduate students in Old Testament and Hebrew helped me do the research. We had combed all the standard lexicons. This is what we found. In Gen. 3:17 the same speaker in the same situation uses the same word as "toil" for Adam which was "pain" for Eve:

> And to Adam he said, "Because you have listened to the voice of your wife, and have eaten of the tree of which I commanded you, 'You shall not eat of it,' cursed is the ground because of you; in *toil* you shall eat of it all the days of your life."

This form of the Hebrew word apparently occurs only in Gen. 3:16,17, and in Gen. 5:29. In Gen. 5:29 "toil" is used and the context would hardly admit the translation "pain." The context in both Gen. 3:17 and Gen. 5:29 is agricultural. All the other cognates of this word in the Old Testament are rendered with words denoting "labor," or sometimes "sorrow" in the psychological rather than physical sense.

There is certainly no mention in Scripture of a "curse" on Eve or women in general with regard to childbearing. In the Old Testament the only women who feel cursed are those who can't bear children. The snake is cursed in Gen., ch. 3, and the ground is cursed, but Adam and Eve are not. In the King James Version, words related to the root *'eṣeb* are translated "sorrow." The word refers to psychological factors—concern, anxiety. In John 16:21 Jesus contrasts the emotion of concern a mother feels before birth (during her labor) with her state of joy afterward. Adam's discipline for his sin is a life of labor instead of ease in paradise. Eve's discipline is also labor. Toil, or labor, is a natural accompaniment of childbirth. Gen. 3:16 indicates that there will be labor for Adam and Eve in this world. There is no reason to attribute pain to women in childbirth on the basis of Gen. 3:16.

Sex in Chapel

Childbirth has continued to be the high point of our life together. In my darkest moments of doubt and depression I remind myself of the goodness of God by thinking of the births of each of our three children. I have learned more and grown more, religiously, from the experience of marriage and parenthood than from any other influence.

One month after we returned to the United States after my graduation, John Mark was born. We didn't know a doctor or a hospital that would allow Sharee to have the delivery without anesthetic and that would allow me to be present. Through the intercession of a good friend, the chief of obstetrics at a distant university hospital took us on. We drove sixty miles over snowy February roads in the middle of the night to get to the hospital. Some of our friends thought we were crazy. We replied that it was simply a question of what you were most afraid of. Sharee and I were more afraid to be separated and to have her unconscious. In the car and at the hospital we were together. This time I had to scrub and gown. But for the rest it was familiar, more calm, a reminder of God's grace—a wonderful experience. Our experience now was not confined to Holland. God was at work wherever we called on him. There were many changes in circumstances while we were expecting our third child. But God gave us confidence in the validity of our experience. Together we saw Toby born, a strong, healthy boy.

I was scheduled to speak in chapel at college the day after Mark was born. I'd been up most of the night and intended to call my friend the chaplain and say I couldn't make it. Sharee suggested: "Why don't you go? You can't lose. They'll forgive you anything today." I was slated to speak on some aspect of current philosophy of religion as part of a series. Naturally I worked the subject around to childbirth. I told of John Mark's birth. Then I announced to the suddenly awake college audience that I knew more about sex than Hugh Hefner! His interests, I asserted, were arrested at the adolescent level—looking at pictures of women's bare breasts. (If young mothers were encouraged to nurse their children—and in public—half the need for *Playboy* would be gone. And young men would have a healthier understanding of sex.) I had just had the experience of going on to adult climax and fulfillment—the birth of our child. I've never given a better-received chapel talk. But it's not one that's easy to repeat!

The good news, the evangelical truth, is that our own experience of God's grace can be a corrective to cultural conservatism. Translators and doctors, like the rest of us, can be locked into our culture. But the truth of God's Word in our own lives can set us free.

CHAPTER 8

Scripture
and Confessions

Every scholar has his own biases. Usually someone does a certain piece of academic research because he wants to prove something. I certainly had something I wanted to prove in my doctoral dissertation. And what an opportunity I had to do it! The subject of my work was Scripture in the Westminster Confession of Faith. I began work on it in 1963, just before beginning my work as a college teacher. The United Presbyterian Church was beginning efforts to prepare a contemporary confession of faith. It was apparently to supplement, or supplant, the Westminster Confession. I wanted to prove that the doctrine of Scripture in the Westminster Confession was orthodox, sound, and still valid. I was sure that the view of the Bible in the proposed Confession of 1967 was heterodox, faulty, and of no help to us.

Seminary Training

I was from the more conservative old United Presbyterian Church of North America, which merged with the Presbyterian Church in the U.S.A. in 1958 to form The United Presbyterian Church in the U.S.A. At seminary I had learned the Anglo-Saxon, American, Presbyterian tradition as Christian orthodoxy. Orthodoxy was defined confessionally by the Westminster Confession of Faith. Orthodoxy was developed theologically in the tradition of Charles Hodge and Benjamin B. Warfield of the old Princeton Theological Seminary. Practically, orthodoxy was defended as the most reasonable understanding of life and reality. We did not analyze the orthodox tradition presented to us. We did not ask where it came from. We presumed that it was the clearest expression of what the Bible in its entirety taught. Our task was to defend it reasonably and to preach it with interesting and practical application. Looking back, I'm sure there were other views and moderating influences. What I have described is the view that seemed to dominate. It is certainly the approach I bought.

My view of the orthodox theology which I had been taught was that it formed an unbroken continuity with the theology of Warfield, the Westminster Confession, Calvin, Augustine, and Paul. All of these, I believed, were treating Scripture in the same way. The proposed Confession of 1967 represented a threat to that identity of tradition. At the request of some area ministers I wrote a critique of the proposed Confession of 1967. My view was very negative, seeing the modern confession as an expression of modern philosophy. I blamed Kant and Kierkegaard as the thinkers whose subjectivism laid the foundation for the new Confession's approach to Scripture. Thus I began my dissertation work with confidence that I understood the issues and with a desire to prove my thesis to others. I felt that modern, unorthodox approaches were changing the church I knew, and I wanted to defend that church, its Scripture, and its confession in a way that was available to me.

Stages of Development

In the summer of 1965 I took a year's leave of absence (which turned into a year and a half) from teaching to finish work on my dissertation. The comedian Victor Borge has a routine in which he announces that the number he has just composed was written in three flats because he moved three times while writing it. My thesis was something like that. My wife and I, with our young son, moved three times, living in three different countries in a search for the sources of Calvinistic orthodoxy.

We first moved to Princeton, New Jersey, for the summer. The events of that summer changed the direction of my thesis. They could well have changed the direction of my life. Opposition to the proposed Confession of 1967 was building. In early July, I traveled to Washington, D.C., and participated in the founding of Presbyterians United for Biblical Confession. The leadership of this group was, to a significant degree, composed of those who had been United Presbyterians before the merger. They were my friends and I was one with their concerns. They later played a significant role in the modification of the Confession of 1967. But all of that took place while I was out of the country finishing my thesis. If I had been in the United States from mid-1965 to early 1967, I would probably have been hard at work with them.

Potentially of even greater significance was a call I received from New York one day that summer. My name had been suggested by a friend as a possible theological adviser to the Presbyterian Lay Committee, then in its initial stages of organization. I took the Princeton commuter train into New York one morning and had lunch with the acting executive secretary of the Lay Committee, and met one of the directors in the offices of his insurance company. They were prepared to offer a full-time paid staff position. My only problem of principle with them was that at this time they were unwilling to enter into debate in the theological arena. They intended to stay away from commenting on the Confession of 1967, for example. I terminated the conversations for practical reasons. I had a teaching job I liked. And most of all, I had a compulsion to finish that dissertation. If I had set the research aside and entered the practical, political arena, my development might have been very different.

My research that summer was carried on at the libraries of Princeton Theological Seminary and Princeton University. It represented a shift of focus from philosophy to history. I intended to do a comparative study of the doctrine of Scripture in the proposed Confession of 1967 and in the Westminster Confession. I went to Princeton because two of the principal authors of the new Confession were resident there: Edward A. Dowey and George S. Hendry. I met with them and read extensively in their writings and those of other members of the drafting committee of the Confession. Dowey suggested, and my research confirmed to me, that the central conflict was primarily a historical one. People were contending for or against a new confession based on their attitude toward the old confession—the Westminster Confession of Faith. What increasingly disturbed me was that those who praised and those who condemned Westminster had one thing in common— they had not studied its sources in their historical setting. Those who praised it were confident that they understood it in the Warfield tradition, and those who opposed it agreed with that interpretation and felt it was not worth further examination. So, after about four months in Princeton we packed our bags and boarded a plane for London.

The British Museum library in London was the one place where virtually all the writings of the Westminster Divines and the historical data on the confession they wrote could be found. In London my attention shifted from doctrines to documents. I had to discover first of all who wrote the chapter on Scripture in the Westminster Confession. There had been some 150 delegates to the Westminster Assembly of Divines, which began meeting at Westminster Abbey in 1643 and continued until 1649. But 150 men do not write a document. I poured over committee records, diaries, and historical accounts. The detective work was fun. From it emerged a group of eleven men, four Scots and seven Englishmen, who appeared to be the primary authors of the Westminster doctrine of Scripture. Then I perused volume after volume of their writings—sermons, tracts, books—seeking everything that related to their doctrine of Scripture.

I knew what I expected to find. My former professor of church history, an ardent advocate of the Westminster Confession, had written a little monograph entitled *A Bible Inerrancy Primer.* In it he reasons from external evidences to the logical conclusion that Scripture is true. Then he commends to us as worthy of acceptance by our heart the truth to which our head has already consented. In this work the author asserts: "That the approach of this Primer was abundantly used by the Westminster divines and seventeenth century Orthodoxy, in general, could be extensively illustrated were there any necessity to prove what no one questions." For six months I read the writings of the Westminster Divines. Not once did I ever find one of them using the method of arguing for the truth of Scripture from external evidences!

The impact of what I had discovered didn't hit me until we had moved back to the Netherlands. There I had to finish writing and publish my dissertation. Month after month I wrote, ten hours a day, six days a week. I would write until 2:00 or 3:00 A.M. and leave a draft for my wife to check and criticize. Meanwhile, she would go to bed about 11:00 P.M. and rise about 6:00 A.M. to do this. I would get up about 9:00 A.M. and within an hour I would be at my desk revising what she had corrected. After lunch I would be ready to begin on a new section. Often in the early hours of the morning I would look at the paper in my typewriter and suddenly ask, "Why did I write that?" I knew I didn't believe that. The reason I had written it was that it was "in the cards." The evidence was there in the thousands of quotations I had copied from the writings of the Westminster Divines. My mind was being changed. What the study of modern theologians had not been able to do for me, the Westminster Divines had done. I was seeing historical dimensions of the doctrine of Scripture that previously I had rejected as modern innovations.

Reformation and Modern Emphases on Scripture

To my shock and surprise, I discovered strong emphases in the Westminster Confession that were not in the tradition I knew. And worse, to my mind, some of these emphases reappeared in the proposed Confession of 1967. The authors of the new Confession were deeply influenced by the neo-Reformation theology of Karl Barth and others who had influenced Presbyterianism in the 1930's and 1940's. That modern neo-Reformation theology had apparently put the authors of the 1967 Confession in touch with Reformation emphases on Scripture that the Westminster Divines had also inherited from Calvin and the Reformers.

The first of these Reformation emphases is that Christ is the central interpretative principle of Scripture. Scripture is not about everything. It is about Jesus Christ and the salvation that he came to offer and effect. There is a main theme in Scripture of God's creation, man's fall into sin, and Christ's redemptive work. That central, saving theme is clear and available to everyone who wants to find it. Biblical critics attacked the historical or scientific accuracy of Scripture judged by modern, Western standards. In response, some theologians such as Warfield attempted to defend Scripture by the same modern standards. Debate on details tended to obscure the centrality of Christ's saving message. Scripture is a religious book, with a religious message. That message is divine. It comes to us in the human form of the witness of real people to their real encounter with God and his saving grace.

One of the most conservative of the eleven principal authors of the Westminster Confession, a Scot, Samuel Rutherford, makes this religious theme clear. Rutherford contends that in general Scripture is our rule, but then he lists several areas in which Scripture is *not* our rule, e.g., "not in things of Art and Science, as to speake Latine, to *demonstrate conclusions of Astronomie.*" Scripture does not intend to instruct us in these areas, according to Rutherford. But he goes on to say of Scripture: "But it is our Rule 1. in fundamentalls of salvation." Edward Reynolds was the most important single figure in framing Westminster's doctrine of Scripture since he alone was on every committee at every stage of the drafting of the document. Reynolds manifests the Divines' commitment to Christ as the Word of God and the Scripture as the Word that reveals him.

Reynolds says: "We may observe how Christ is frequently pleased to honour his gospel with his own titles and attributes. And therefore the apostle speaks of him and his word, as of one and the same thing."

The other principal Reformation emphasis in both the Westminster Confession and the 1967 confession is that the Holy Spirit moves us to accept Scripture's authority. We do not first need to demonstrate the rational acceptability of Scripture and then seek the Holy Spirit to move our hearts. The Spirit was present in the production of Scripture, inspiring those who wrote it. Equally, the Spirit is present in those who hear or read Scripture, persuading them of its authority. This persuasion is not directed to human hearts alone, but is applied to the total human personality, in which head and heart interact inseparably. The fear of mysticism by Warfield and the old Princeton theologians and the fear of existentialism by contemporary conservative evangelicals apparently led to suppression of this subjective dimension. The Princeton theologians relied heavily on the philosophy of Scottish Realism. Rational certainty was put before the inner testimony of the Holy Spirit regarding Scripture's authority.

The Reformers and the Westminster Divines were no more afraid of subjectivism than they were of rationalism. They always sought the balance of accepting Scripture by the persuasion of the Spirit and understanding it by the use of reason and evidence. Always Christ and his saving message stood at the center of what they accepted and how they interpreted it. Very striking is the attitude of Samuel Rutherford, who seems at times to be the most rationally oriented of the Westminster Divines. I remember my excitement when reading a tract of Rutherford's against the Roman Catholics. I came to a section that asks: How do we know that Scripture is the Word of God? Now, I thought, finally I will get the rational argument, the objective proof from external evidences, a refutation of the scholastics on their own terms. Instead, Rutherford appeals to our subjective awareness! For him, the Spirit of Christ speaks to us in Scripture.

> Sheep are docile creatures, Ioh. 10.27. *My sheep heare my voyce, I know them, and they follow me. . . .* so the instinct of Grace knoweth the voyce of the Beloved amongst many voyces, *Cant.* 2.8. and this discerning power is *in the Subject.*

That is it! The sheep know the voice of the shepherd. The subject hears Christ's voice, and believes. Edward Reynolds evidences the same emphasis in what he writes. For Reynolds, the Spirit is the Spirit of Christ who works in the Word to persuade us.

> Which should teach us what to look for in the *Ministry of the Word,* namely that which will convince us, that which puts an edge upon the Word, and opens the heart and makes it burn, namely, the Spirit *of Christ; for by that only we can be brought unto the righteousness of Christ.*

It is not a formal argument for the divine form of the Bible on which the Reformers and the Divines relied for persuasion. They were convinced that when men encountered the person of Christ, the Spirit would bring them into a personal relationship to him. As men trusted Christ, so they would trust the book that witnessed to him. For the Reformers and the Divines, the Word of God is not only the Bible but also preaching based on Scripture. Both the written and the spoken Word witness to the living Word, in whom is salvation.

The Lessons of History

The Reformers relied on a personal relationship to Christ to give Scripture its authority. They had also seen Scripture, not as a general encyclopedia of information, but as a religious book with a central, saving message. Where then had the need for rational objectivity and the fear of subjectivism come from in the orthodox tradition? Commitment to certain philosophical forms as essential to Christian faith apparently screened out some elements of the Biblical witness. When we feel our faith threatened, it is natural that we turn in search of some objective certainty. At the same time we must be clear that neither Augustine, nor Calvin, nor Luther, nor the framers of the Westminster Confession predicated their trust in Scripture on rational evidences of its divinity. Rather, they were compelled by the unique person of Christ and his unique message of salvation to have confidence in the trustworthiness of sources that witnessed to him.

It is always harder for the second generation to hold on to the purity of insight of reformers, be they Calvin or the Westminster Divines. The sixteenth-century Reformation was threatened by the Roman Catholic counterreformation. In the late seventeenth century in Europe, the followers of the Reformers responded by taking up the weapons of the Roman Catholics. Protestant scholastics used the logic of Aristotle to defend the Protestant position against Thomistic arguments. In response to Roman Catholic reliance on the subjective authority of the church to give authority to Scripture, Protestants sought a certain, objective authority in the inspired Scripture itself. In the late seventeenth century in Switzerland that Protestant defensive movement came to a climax in a confession written by Francis Turretin. That confession claimed that even the vowel points in the Hebrew manuscript of the Old Testament were inspired. What Turretin did not know, or overlooked, was that Hebrew as originally written did not even have the grammatical helps known as vowel points!

Similarly, in the nineteenth century, the old Princeton theology of Hodge and Warfield was threatened by the Biblical criticism that was being imported from Germany to America. Instead of relying (as the Reformers and the Westminster Divines had relied) on the Spirit to authenticate the trustworthiness of a Christ-proclaiming Scripture, the old Princeton theologians attempted to meet the critics on the critics' own grounds. When contemporary standards of historical and scientific accuracy were used to criticize the Bible's trustworthiness, Warfield and his followers attempted to defend Scripture's accuracy by the same standards. The fact that the saving message of Scripture had been given in ancient times and in Near Eastern culture was pushed into the background in the desire to defend the contemporary reliability, not of Scripture's content, but of its *form*. Significantly—while verbal assent was given to the Westminster Confession and while its articles were logically defended, the basic theological system studied at the old Princeton Seminary was the theology of Francis Turretin.

What About Us?

In defending the faith, one is easily led into recasting the faith to conform with the current questions being asked of it. Warfield felt the Bible to be threatened by science and he tried to make the Bible's validity scientifically provable. In doing so, he diverted attention from the prescientific, religious purpose of Scripture and raised doubts about its authenticity by asking questions that it was never intended to answer.

Some contemporary defenders of the faith feel that Scripture is threatened by interpretations rising out of a Kantian philosophical framework. Kant denied metaphysics and declared that the thing-in-itself could never be known. He shifted scholars' attention to the question: How is knowledge possible? Many contemporary conservative evangelicals are wholly absorbed with the problem of knowledge, as I was. In trying to defend Scripture from Kantian attack as I did, they have conceived it as a book of knowledge intended to give valid information on every subject directly or indirectly. As a defender of the faith I felt that an inerrant Bible could solve the difficult Kantian problem of knowledge and assure that we can have valid rational and objective answers to our intellectual questions. But is that what God is trying to give us? In attempting thus to defend Scripture, do we not risk diverting attention from its actual form and obscuring its saving content? The Bible is not a computer printout of concise technical information. It is more like an ancient drama, the setting and sequence of which is often strange to us. Yet the miracle of understanding continues to occur in every generation. Men and women encounter in the Bible's pages a Person whose words and deeds meet our central human needs. The power of the Holy Spirit, working through the non-Western, prescientific form of Scripture, continually meets the basic need of the most contemporary person —the need to be saved and to become a new and increasingly whole human being. Scripture answers this basic need—but not by pointing to a new principle, whether scientific or philosophical. It points rather to a person, Jesus Christ. What the Bible offers is not proofs but a Person to persuade us. The ordination vows for ministers in the United Presbyterian

Church bid us do our work in an evangelical perspective: ". . . in obedience to Jesus Christ, under the authority of the Scriptures, and under the continuing instruction and guidance of the confessions."

CHAPTER 9

Evangelical Social Action

The year 1967 was particularly poignant for me. That year marked the beginning of a significant change in my own understanding of Christian social concern. I thought of myself as a conservative evangelical. Through the varied experiences of college, seminary, and graduate school, I had assented to the thesis that the primary task of the church was to evangelize individuals. My theological interest was to defend a traditional conservative position and show how inadequate the liberal options were. Regarding societal problems, I was quite suspicious of, even hostile toward, most of the social pronouncements and activities of my denomination. My voting record as a citizen was consistent with my generally conservative stance; I voted for Eisenhower against Stevenson, Nixon against Kennedy, and Goldwater against Johnson.

In 1967 two experiences combined to challenge and change me. My dissertation research had changed me, almost against my will. The conservative theological position that I had defended as *the* Christian faith was of nineteenth-century origin, very culturally conditioned, and in some ways an inadequate response to the present time. I had to begin rethinking my theology. In the summer of 1967 I was invited by a Wisconsin church to give a series of lectures over the Labor Day weekend on the topic "How Should the Church Meet Change?" As I wrestled with current changes in my own denomination— confessional, liturgical, ecumenical, and those involving social action—my mind began to change. The more I worked with the problems, the more convinced I became that denominational leaders weren't so bad. For the most part they were making responsible, creative, and Christian responses to the complex problems presented us by changing times. I couldn't have done better.

Unbiblical Assumptions

As I reflect on these changes in my own life I have come to a disturbing hypothesis. I offer it to you and suggest that you test it in your own experience. The hypothesis is this: we conservative evangelicals are not consistently Biblical when we approach social problems. We shift ground from dependence on Scripture for our norms and models to "practicality," "realism," and an uncritical acceptance of the world's standards. Several times I have given a series of lectures under the title "The Apostles' Creed and Contemporary Social Problems." The audience reaction follows a consistent pattern. While I give a historical treatment of how the creed developed and its meaning, there is polite interest. As I present an exegesis of the Scriptural passages lying behind a particular creedal section, you can see nodding approval of this Biblical emphasis. When I go on to apply the Biblically interpreted creedal statement to a social problem, suddenly the audience response changes— often to icy indifference or active hostility. Conservative evangelical audiences don't just disagree with my interpretations. They sometimes question the legitimacy of making any application of our Biblical and creedal theology to social problems. Christians take offense when a discussion of God the Father Almighty and the Biblical meaning of might and power is connected with a discussion of this country's use of its armed might and power. Similarly, we can apply exegesis to Scripture passages regarding the first-century meaning of Jesus Christ, his only Son our Lord. But it is considered wrong to ask the question of who or what we make to be our lord in the twentieth century, especially if the question of American wealth is related to the issue of world poverty.

I still have deep feelings about two experiences in this regard. In the late 1960's many college campuses were fermenting with protest movements. Our small college was not. I often commented that if my whole mission in life had been to cause a revolution on our campus, I don't think I could have brought it off. The area church people, however, were much agitated by what they read in the papers about campus unrest. Our chaplain was asked to speak at a Methodist church one Sunday evening on "The Student Revolution." He discovered a conflict in schedule and asked me to take his place. Since I didn't know any more than what everyone read in the papers, I didn't know what to do. At that time I did have one student with a red beard who was writing a paper on the philosophy of the radical SDS (Students for a Democratic Society) for my philosophy class. So I took him with me. He was very concerned to make a good impression. He trimmed his beard, wore his best suit, and was exceedingly polite. He wasn't an SDS member himself. The people didn't mind him at all. But some of them were very angry with me for suggesting that we should take him seriously. One man in the front row became very agitated. He told me in no uncertain terms that I was a disgrace to the college and shouldn't be allowed to teach. That was unpleasant. The aftermath was even more devastating. I discovered through a friend that I was being investigated. My antagonist turned out to be the county district attorney. Nothing came of the investigation, but a few weeks later he got newspaper publicity by announcing to the DAR that he knew the cause of campus violence. It was the radical college professors!

Later in the spring I was invited to speak at a Wednesday evening covered-dish dinner at a large Presbyterian church. The topic? You guessed it: "The Student Revolution." As I left the house that night I said to Sharee: "Don't worry. This time I'm going to be smart. I'm not getting into any trouble." And I tried not to. I went and met some very nice people, mostly of middle age, well up in their businesses and professions. I gave a standard, rather dull, speech of mine. I spoke about Plato and Aristotle and their differing notions of change in this world. I mentioned Jesus and his attitude toward change. Then I concluded with only one sentence about "the student revolution." I said: "Perhaps we should listen to the students, for they may be posing problems with which we will need to deal." I swear that's all I said. But that was enough! The vice-president of an insurance company called me a Communist. The director of the local YMCA shook his fist at me and said: "I'd like to get you down in the gym and work you over." At that time there seemed to be no way to get American church people to consider this very threatening area. I quit trying. I never spoke on that topic again.

What causes this strange inconsistency? Why should we who profess acceptance of the whole Bible be so insensitive to its social and cultural mandates? I believe that the root cause lies in a tradition of theological interpretation. We read the Bible through the eyes of Western, especially American, culture. Let us be clear on this: we all interpret the Bible. As soon as you do anything besides just quoting Bible verses you are interpreting. Even quoting verses involves an interpretation—governed by the translation you choose, which verses you select, and in what order you select them. All people, including those who claim to take the Bible literally, frequently bring to its interpretation assumptions uncritically accepted from our culture. The culture we live in has been programming us since we were born. Unless we are radically self-critical, we can easily interpret Scripture in ways more in harmony with our culture than with the central thrust of the Biblical message.

Let me suggest three unbiblical assumptions often brought to Scripture by American Christians. The first assumption is that God deals primarily with individuals. This makes sense to us in individualistic America. But it would, for cultural reasons, hardly have occurred to a Hebrew. In the Old Testament there is a strong emphasis on the unity of mankind and an especial emphasis on the solidarity of the convenant community. Families living in tents and moving as clans would have found it most difficult to imagine God to be interested only in individuals. There is no private "prayer closet" in a tent. A second unbiblical assumption is that there are two great separated realms, the sacred and the secular; that Biblical norms rule the first and civil norms rule the second. On the contrary, in the Hebrew view there is one universe and it is God's. God is not only the creator, he is the redeemer of the whole world. He is not intent on snatching people out of the world as brands from the burning. He is interested in making persons and their environment whole. A third unbiblical assumption is that those in authority are always to be obeyed as instruments of God. Christians often isolate Rom., ch. 13, and take it out of the context of the whole of Scripture. According to one of the main themes of Scripture, however, to make any person or thing absolute except God himself is idolatry. "Israel—Love It or Leave It" was certainly not a slogan the prophets could have accepted. Because they loved their nation and their people they were constantly criticizing them and calling them to repentance. Jesus' disciples were acutely aware that conflicts could arise between allegiance to God and loyalty to earthly authorities. When such conflicts occurred, the disciples found it necessary to obey God rather than men (Acts 4:19; 7:51–53; 12:6–11).

These three examples of unbiblical assumptions are meant to raise the suspicion that cultural conservatism may often be uncritically imposed on our evangelical Christianity. Too often we comfortably think of ourselves as conservative evangelicals. In such a combination it is possible not only that the first word grammatically modifies the second but that our conservatism can dominate and mute our evangelicalism.

As a test of the thesis stated above, let us examine several examples of contemporary social problems in which the application of evangelical assumptions made me very uncomfortable with my formerly unquestioned cultural conservatism.

Race

Several years ago I spoke on "Black Theology" as part of a series on contemporary trends in theology. The audience was composed of about fifty white people. Also present were two black pastors, seated in the front row. The previous day I had observed the interaction of a white audience and a black theologian, James Cone. I was depressed. The estrangement I felt between the whites and Cone was awful. I felt that a white man had no constructive role to play in the present racial situation. I wasn't yet willing to assume the responsibility that Cone proposed—complete identification with oppressed black people. Nevertheless, I was determined to present black theology as much as possible from a black man's perspective. I knew that I couldn't fully do justice to it. I went to speak. I made no criticism of black theology at all. I presented the main argument of Cone's early work, *Black Theology and Black Power* (Seabury, 1969). I presented the black criticism of white theology and the white church, and I confessed my own sins. Confessing real sin was hard to do in front of a white, upper-middle-class audience with two black men sitting in the front row. My confession was hard for the white audience to accept. After the opening question in the discussion period, the conversation shifted to the two black pastors interacting with the white audience. I went to one side and sat down, feeling emotionally exhausted. One of the black men, a pastor and professor (with two Ph.D.'s), took over the discussion. He concluded it with a presentation so profound and so moving that it made me feel like a little boy. The biggest surprise was still to come. That brilliant black theologian said: "The real issue is human liberation. We need to get beyond the point of seeing things in terms of race and go on to seek freedom for all people." If I had said that, any black theologian would have rightly objected that I was avoiding the real issue—that of identifying with the needs of an oppressed minority. I learned something important that evening. The thing a white person can do is admit to other white people that the race problem is really a white problem. I can confess that I am a white racist—unwillingly, beginning to repent, but still not at the point of really identifying with the oppressed in a manner sufficient for them to judge me to be one of them. That isn't much. But it is where I am. Maybe it is where you are. I hope it is the beginning of new directions for us.

Nationalism

Racism and nationalism are often closely linked. The near-elimination of the American Indians was justified by continual appeal to the cultural superiority and manifest destiny of white Europeans to rule this continent. The government conveniently sent Christian missionaries along with military contingents when it was time to break another treaty and take away more of the land that had been promised to the red man forever. Such standard American aphorisms as "The only good Indian is a dead Indian" and "Gooks don't count" must be actively challenged lest Christians passively support their validity. My Lai is possible for a nation that has never really faced up to and repented for what happened at Sand Creek Canyon and Wounded Knee. (See Dee Brown's *Bury My Heart at Wounded Knee: An Indian History of the American West;* Holt, Rinehart & Winston, 1971).

Surely we in America are no more exempt from the danger of allowing unquestioned obedience to the state to take the place of obedience to God than were the ancient Israelites. The Old Testament prophets and the New Testament apostles were much less fearful of anarchy and lawlessness than they were offended by the demonic pretensions of the authoritarian state. Our oversimplified and inaccurate view of the principal struggle in the world blinds Christians as well as other Americans to this issue. We sometimes think the single issue of our time is the struggle between Communism and our form of democracy. That very comfortable view of the world puts us automatically and irrevocably on the right side as long as we have nothing to do with Communism. Of equal importance are the struggles between the rich and the poor, the strong and the weak, the white and the nonwhite. To face these realities is not so comforting. Americans are cast in the role of the minority and the oppressor in each instance. Even less comforting is the nagging suspicion that the priorities of Third World peoples on these issues are probably closer to the Biblical view of reality.

Wealth

The gospel of Jesus Christ is not neutral to sociopolitical realities. We praise and reward those who have wealth and power. The gospel is clearly biased in favor of the poor and the oppressed. Jesus was asked the fundamental religious question: "What shall I do to inherit eternal life?" He responded to the rich young ruler by telling him that orthodoxy and personal morality were not enough. That young man's ultimate value was apparently his standard of living. Jesus had to tell him to sell what he had and give it to the poor—if he wished to be saved. That is surely applicable to us who live in what is by far the richest nation on the earth. On another occasion a religious lawyer asked an insincere question to test Jesus: "Teacher, what shall I do to inherit eternal life?" Jesus responded by telling the story of the good Samaritan. This story has special poignancy for me as a practicing religious professional. My predecessors, the priest and the Levite, passed by the beaten and half-dead man without helping him. The equivalent of the Samaritan in our day could be a poor black man who came along in his 1939 Ford and took time to stop and minister to the needs of the beaten man.

We need a theology of liberation. The oppressed may understand portions of the gospel that we don't heed. Those who have suffered privation are moved more quickly to minister to the deprived. The Biblical notion of the unity of the human race and especially the New Testament concept of the body of Christ must shake us out of our individualism and make us aware of our responsibilities to our brothers and sisters.

Women

Recently I was the professor related to a course on the theology of women's liberation. Some of the student wives at our seminary had been requesting more attention to their particular role in the community. The husbands of some of them were on the student council and requested me to teach a course on the subject of women's liberation. (Notice who had the power and who decided on the proper action!) Our only woman faculty member had retired, so I took the assignment. My theory was that it was better to do something poorly than not to do it at all. Six students signed up to take the course for credit. The first night of the course fifty-eight persons came, nearly all of them women. Each night for the following nine weeks the group averaged more than fifty women. Almost all of them were there because they had a personal stake in what was being discussed. They were hurting. The openness and honesty of these people from the beginning surpassed that of participants in any group of similar size that I had worked with. One of the student wives gave focus to the feelings of many: "In my experience with the Bible, I can't believe that God wants me to be what women have become. I can't accept the traditional interpretation of the woman's place. But I know God and believe that the Bible is imperative for the growth of my faith. There must be a point where these come together. I want to find it."

I didn't "teach" that course. I convened, moderated, communicated data from outside sources, and invited those with expertise to share it. Value judgments and ethical decisions were referred to the women. As a group we empathized and identified with the concerns of the women's liberation movement. I offered no critique. Letting women lead was difficult for me as a man, but it was demanded by the situation. Admitting that I was a white racist was one thing. Discovering that I was an unconscious sexist was added pain.

Jesus was a feminist. He radically treated women as persons in ways shocking to his culture. The gospel records make that clear. In one of Jesus' parables, the parable of the lost coin, a *woman* stands as a symbol for *God*. By choosing that illustration, our Lord must have knowingly scandalized the Jewish religious community. A prayer to be recited by Jewish males included thanks that one was not created a Gentile, a slave, or a woman. By contrast, the apostle Paul affirmed the radical equality of all Christians: "There is neither Jew nor Greek, there is neither slave nor free, there is neither male nor female; for you are all one in Christ Jesus" (Gal. 3:28). At the same time, Paul's culture was not open to the liberation of women any more than it was prepared for the elimination of slavery.

As a missionary pastor, Paul urged conformity to culture where necessary. We make the distinction between central Biblical affirmations and their cultural application when we distinguish, for example, between the moral and the ceremonial law. Yet how easy it is for us, with our conservative bias, to absolutize Paul's culture. We need instead to affirm the gospel of equality and liberation as Paul did. Evangelical Christians especially should be sensitive to the gospel's demands for our time and culture. They should not seek to justify the subordination of women today by appealing to the mores of a past society.

Ecology

The Christian faith is often blamed for our ecological crisis. In *The New York Times,* January 4, 1970, Edward B. Fiske wrote of "The Link Between Faith and Ecology." According to Fiske, the environmentalists level two basic charges against the Christian faith. The first charge is that Christianity is excessively individualistic. Salvation is understood as a relationship between God and the individual with no connection to his relationship with other persons or the world. That notion is utterly unbiblical. Certainly a Hebrew could never have thought in narrowly individualistic terms. We as Christians must nevertheless admit that the Greek philosophical mold into which our theology has often been cast has given rise to a kind of "pie in the sky by and by" Platonism. We have too often allowed this one-sided philosophy to pass as genuine Christianity. The second charge is that Christianity is excessively otherworldly. The Christian God is held to be a holy, transcendent being who has no relationship with and little concern (if any) for this world. Again, the Biblical data clearly contradict this charge. Our God created this world. One could say God likes dirt—he made it! God's concern—his love—for the world is manifested especially in the incarnation. God came himself. His Son became one of us and shared in our environment. The God of the Bible is not the same as his creation. But he is intimately and lovingly involved with it at every moment.

The word "ecology" comes from the Greek word *oikos,* meaning "house," and pertains to our environment. From the same Greek word we get "ecumenical," i.e., pertaining to the whole household of God. The Bible views the whole environment as the household, the creation, the dwelling place of God.

The trouble is, we have read Gen. 1:26, where God grants dominion over the earth, as a carte blanche to do what we please. It is really a contract giving us responsibility to care for the Father's property. Man as created is both one with all other created things in nature and made in a special relationship to God. That special relationship is one of responsiveness and responsibility. The central text for our understanding of the environment should be: "The Lord God took the man and put him in the garden of Eden to till it and keep it" (Gen. 2:15). Our culture allows concern for the profit of oil companies to predominate over concern for poison in the air that children breathe. That can scarcely be classified as responsibly fulfilling God's cultural mandate. It is evangelical to care for the earth.

Unsettled Axioms

The preceding illustrations challenged many of my conservative axioms. Axioms are assumptions we take for granted to be true. We must learn to unsettle those settled axioms and to rethink our most basic concepts. Then we need to develop an evangelical theology of social change.

One of the most encouraging signs is that evangelicals are beginning to do this. "A Declaration of Evangelical Social Concern," which came from the 1973 Thanksgiving weekend meeting of forty evangelical leaders, is one significant manifestation. Another is the spate of books now being produced by evangelicals on a wide range of social issues. This comes at a time when the liberal wing of the church seems tired and in need of retrenchment. An alumnus of a prestigious Eastern seminary told me of a West Coast alumni meeting with the president of his alma mater. This liberal theologian was decrying the fact that he saw little sign of social concern in the

present student body. The only course that drew a large enroll-
ment was a course on monastic piety, taught by a Roman
Catholic. My friend, relating the incident, commented: "I
suppose you at Fuller are making hay in this current trend. I
suppose your students have been mostly into personal piety all
along." I was glad to point out one of the values of conservatism. Because we had never been wholly caught up in the
social-action syndrome, we were not now in a state of reaction
against it. We have always had students whose principal concern was personal religion. We have had, and continue to have,
a significant number of students with a central concern for
applying the gospel in society. In a modest way, these groups
and others cross-fertilize and inform each other. Evangelicals
are working at finding a balance, perhaps now more than ever
before. But the task is far from done. We must test whether
our assumptions are derived from the gospel of Jesus Christ or
whether they are simply derived from elements of our culture
and imposed on the gospel.

Let's reconsider several fundamental questions. One is the
nature of authority. In my experience, individual Christians
and the organized church have often accepted and sanctioned
the use of coercive and legalistic means as the proper expression
of authority. Scripture, especially our Lord's example, presents
a different concept of authority. Christ's authority is that of his
person. He is inherently persuasive and powerful rather than
externally legal and authoritarian. He had no authority except
that his truth answered persons' questions and his acts met
their needs. Consider also the nature of Biblical truth. The
gospel nowhere sanctifies the rigid, formal patterns of Greek
logic. In the Bible, truth is personal, relational. Jesus says, "I
am the way, and the *truth*, and the life" (John 14:6). Consider
further the nature of society. The Bible commends no one style

of life. It does not absolutize the way of life sanctioned by the majority in a culture—especially not when that culture is materialistic, individualistic, and selfish. God's good world is presented as a world of infinite variety, where persons with differences can be treated as equally valuable. All persons are responsible ultimately to God and not to our systems.

The above considerations of assumptions, applications, and axioms are not intended to lay down definitive pronouncements. They are meant to raise genuine questions. These questions haunt me as I teach systematic theology and try to live as a husband, father, and citizen. I hope they will disturb you in your work and life. I hope they will drive us, together, as evangelical Christians, to a renewed, fresh, and self-critical search of Scripture. We must interpret the gospel message with a corrected bias. We must apply it to the needs of our society with a courageous boldness. God has not called us to be just conservatives. We must conserve the very best in our heritage, to be sure. But our primary concern should not simply be to protect and preserve the ideas and institutions of the past. God has called us to be evangelicals. We need to hear the good news of Jesus Christ in the present. We need to heed that good news in action which changes persons and uses culture for Christian purposes. If we can correct our biases toward individualism, toward compartmentalization into sacred and secular, and toward prideful nationalism; if we can forsake false idealizations and be our real selves, applying the real Scripture to the real world; then we can offer good news—not proof texts for the privileged but the whole gospel for the healing of God's whole world.

CHAPTER 10

Afterthoughts
on Apologetics

When I was invited to join the faculty at Fuller Theological Seminary I was doubtful. I hesitated to leave the context of a college faculty with Christians working in widely diverse fields. I feared that a seminary might be a kind of ghetto where everyone had to think alike and talk the same lingo. Fortunately my fears were unfounded. Fuller is an interdenominational school. That helps. We necessarily recognize the validity of differing traditions. We constantly confront one another as sincere scholars who can differ on matters of interpretation. And yet we can work together as those who share a common evangelical faith and relationship to Christ.

There is another factor that helps enormously: Fuller Theological Seminary is not just one, but three schools. In addition to the School of Theology there are two other graduate schools: the School of Psychology and the School of World Mission. The faculty and students in these schools share the evangelical faith and relationship to Christ. But they think in different categories. And they use different scholarly language. They are applying the insights of the behavioral sciences to the healing of distressed personalities and to the understanding of diverse cultures. Fuller is no ghetto!

My anthropologist friends have helped me to understand the role that my conservative culture has played in forming my theology. My psychologist friends have helped me to deal with the internal tensions arising from my struggles within myself and with my background. As I look back at what I have written I know that this book could not have been written without those Christian friends.

Love and Anger

I look back at my past in love and anger. I look back in love because it was my conservative family and church which brought me to Christ and nurtured me as a person. But I also look back in anger because of the unnecessary problems, hang-ups, and restrictions on the gospel which I imbibed from that conservatism.

Why can't we have the Christian message without the cultural mess-ups? I want to enter into discussion with my contemporary conservative evangelical friends on that question. I fear that some of the most popular and widely read and heard apologists are creating the same problems in sincere young Christians now that my background created in me. I encounter evangelical students coming into my classes every day with these problems. These students are bright, committed to Christ, and from the center of the mainstream denominations. But many of them have adopted viewpoints much narrower than historic evangelical Christendom. Apologists traditionally are those concerned to defend the Christian faith from misunderstanding and communicate it in contemporary thought forms. I understand that as my task, too. My debate with conservative evangelical apologists is an intramural one. It is between Christian brothers. It is not a discussion that would even interest someone who did not share our common concern to be Biblical in our thought and life. But that is why the discussion is so serious. We are talking about truth that matters in life. I wouldn't dare speak in this area except that I've said and done everything about which I'm now raising questions.

Philosophy and Theology

Most of the controversy among conservative evangelical apologists is really over philosophy. We don't differ so much on what the Bible says. The issues are joined on what philosophical stance is necessary to interpret and communicate the message. I've taught philosophy for over ten years. I always deal with schools of thought. In Western philosophy the first school is Classical Realism. Its founders were Plato and Aristotle. There were significant differences between them. But on two basic points they agreed. First, there is a real world out there. Second, it can be known by the human mind. The two philosophers split on the nature of that world and how it could best be known. Plato thought that reality was ideas, or ideals, outside of this world. Knowledge of these great ideas is innate, born into us. From the great ideas all other knowledge could be deduced. Aristotle thought that reality was concrete things in the world. By examining enough individual things we could inductively come to true generalizations.

The goal that Plato and Aristotle shared was certain knowledge of an objective world. The validity of both their methods is evidenced by the great schools of Western thought that followed each of them. The medieval world was dominated by the thought of Augustine, who followed Plato, and Thomas Aquinas, who followed Aristotle. There were of course other voices. The mystics said that God could be known directly, experientially. Duns Scotus and William of Occam were skeptical about whether finite humans could have certain knowledge about objective reality at all. Luther, in his reaction to Thomas and Aristotle, said: "I am of Occam's school." But generally the first-generation Reformers followed Augustine. Their second-generation followers returned to the scholasticism of Thomas and Aristotle.

In the seventeenth century the split in Western thought became decisive. Descartes took the Platonic tradition and ran away with it. He began from one great idea he found within himself: "I think, therefore I am." From that he claimed to deduce the knowledge of all of reality. During the seventeenth century his direction was followed by Spinoza and finally Leibniz, who deduced that this was the best of all possible worlds. The effort to gain certain knowledge of reality by the reason alone petered out in absurdity. Voltaire's *Candide* expressed the intellectuals' reaction to Leibniz.

In the eighteenth century John Locke led a massive reaction to rationalism. He chose to follow the lead of the Aristotelian inductive tradition. He determined to find certain knowledge of everything based on sense experience alone. An Irish Anglican bishop, George Berkeley, followed his lead. The logic of this position was finally worked out at the end of the century by David Hume. His answer: Skepticism! On the basis of sense experience alone no certain knowledge was possible.

The contemporary period in philosophy began with Immanuel Kant. He faced the debacle of two centuries of trying to gain certain knowledge of objects by reason or by experience. Kant laid the groundwork for modern science and philosophy by two great insights. First, absolutely certain knowledge of objects is not possible for humans. We can describe how things appear to us, but we cannot know finally what their essence is.

Secondly, both reason and experience are necessary for knowledge. Sense experience provides the data, the facts. Reason provides the mental categories by which we make coherent sense of our experience. Space and time, cause and effect, are not things but categories in our minds. They are concepts by which we commonly make sense out of the variety of our experience.

Kant called this the Copernican revolution in philosophy. Copernicus discovered that the sun did not revolve around the earth. The church condemned Galileo when he expressed that same view. In the eyes of a conservative church, Galileo's main fault was that he began from his own observations rather than beginning from Aristotle's philosophy.

Kant's Copernican revolution turns our attention from the objective world outside to what we subjectively bring to it. We cannot know the essence of objects, but only how they appear to us. And the most important elements in life—values, purposes, and the presence of God—are not known objectively, but personally. We need not accept all of Kant's ideas. We can deplore his absolute separation of facts from values. But may we not be grateful for the main thrust of his thought? All reality is not known in the same way. Sense experience and reason are appropriate ways of describing objects. Persons, values, and purposes are known through personal relationship and practical application in life. Knowing a loving God is more like knowing a loving wife or husband than like knowing a board or a beetle. No scientific research can prove or disprove the Spirit-God's existence or his attitude toward us. No theoretical study will tell us the meaning of life. The message of the gospel tells us of a God we can know personally. The gospel proclaims meaning and purpose which can be tested and validated in life.

As conservative evangelical apologists, we often condemn

Kant for his revolution just as medieval churchmen condemned Copernicus for his. Yet, as evangelicals, dare we be blind to the values that have resulted from Kant's insights? The modern behavioral sciences became possible. No longer do psychologists wrangle over man's essence—they describe how he behaves and they seek ways of healing his destructive behaviors. Anthropologists can take serious account of the relative character of human cultures. They can value the useful function that each culture plays without asking which culture is absolutely correct, or divinely sanctioned. Descriptions by behavioral scientists of man's functions in society do not pretend to answer the fundamental value questions: What is a human self? Are persons free? Is there purpose and meaning in life? The answers we bring to those questions come from our faith. For Christians they come from our Biblically informed faith. Faith is not opposed to fact. But faith enables us to trust in persons and to know purposes that are more than a sum of facts. Theology reflects on the Biblical message, with its central concern for man's salvation. And theology tries to work out the implications of what the Bible says about a person's selfhood, freedom, and purpose.

I think acceptance of the values of Kant's revolution frees us from trying to prove scientifically things we can not and need not prove. Biblical scholars have long known that the first eleven chapters of Genesis are theological, not scientific, information. That God is the creator and that his creation is good in origin but marred by man's sin, only Scripture could tell us. The central, saving message of a redeemer roots in Gen. 3:15. The implications of the theological message of Genesis relate to the meaning of life, our purposes and values. The rest of Scripture is like a drama in which this central theme of creation, fall, and redemption is developed and brought to its focus in the life, death, and resurrection of Christ.

The processes by which God created the world and the historical details of Israel's existence can be investigated by normal scientific methods. Through the sciences we can learn much of value about the human context in which the Biblical revelation is given. But the meaning of the Biblical message can only be received in faith and validated in life. The sciences have no techniques for knowing God or establishing the meaning and purpose of our lives. God's personhood is not only infinite and thus more than our finite personhood. God is a Spirit and thus is different from us. His self-revelation in the God-man Jesus Christ is meant to save us, not to satisfy our scientific curiosity.

Apologetic Witness

As apologists we would like the persuasive power of objective, certain knowledge. But Biblically the desire for objective human security has often been branded idolatry. Reasonable proofs can be our golden calf. We feel anxious, as the Israelites did when Moses was out of their sight. Like them we need to wait for God's Word rather than substitute something we can see and understand and control. None of the traditional rational proofs for God's existence are logically conclusive. There are counterevidences for all the usual Christian evidences used to prove the truth of our faith. If we offer these human constructions to people as the basis of their faith, we are giving them a destructible golden calf.

Neither rationalist "presuppositional apologetics" nor empiricist "evidential apologetics" really prove the Christian position. Both are helpful. They offer logic and evidence that can clear away misunderstandings and support believers' faith. I believe that all forms of apologetics are really sophisticated forms of witness. The apologist by his arguments communicates to his hearers the depth and importance of his own relationship to Jesus Christ. I thank God for the way he uses our diverse systems and styles. The fact that God uses us doesn't sanctify our theories. It only affirms his grace.

In every period of history and every culture in the world the gospel message has given new life, meaning, and purpose to people. They have not thought alike nor viewed the same evidences. But the Spirit of God has given them an experiential, personal knowledge of Christ.

We must ask ourselves: must all people become pre-Kantian before they can become Christian? Surely that is not the case. God is not an absolute idea or an empirical object to be known among other ideas or objects. God is a person who is known in the dynamic of personal relationship—which cannot be analyzed scientifically.

I fear that to some extent our apologetics reverses the Biblical relationship between the Holy Spirit's work and our responsibility. The Reformers affirmed the Biblical teaching that the Holy Spirit saves. We don't convert people. God will use our witness, imperfect as it is. The Spirit uses the gospel wherever it is preached—even, as Paul notes, when preached out of wrong motives; and even, as we all know, when supported by weak reasons and evidences. The Holy Spirit brings a person to faith in Christ. An aspect of that faith is the inner witness of the Holy Spirit that the Biblical record is authoritative. The witness to the living Word, Jesus Christ, is the written Word of God. We usually come to believe in them both at the same time. Then, according to the Reformers, our reason, with all the evidence we can muster, comes into play in interpreting the Scripture.

I'm also concerned when we apologists seem to reverse the roles of the Holy Spirit and our reason. Some conservative evangelicals seem to feel that the authority of the Word and the facts about Christ must be proved before the Spirit can work. Then someone who has become a Christian, instead of being freed to use the power of reason to look at the evidence, is asked to step into a conservative knowledge-ghetto. The Christian is asked to deny the consensus of modern scholarship in philosophy. Everything since Kant is judged to be basically wrong. Saying that all of modern philosophy is wrong because it claims "autonomy" doesn't help either. The claim to autonomy, while false, does not eliminate valuable insights in modern thought. To claim that only a particular conservative view of the history of philosophy can be correct unfortunately appears to be some kind of claim to autonomy as well.

Evaluating the Evidence

Generally there are two criteria by which apologetic effort is judged: (1) Is it comprehensive? Does it deal with all the facts? and (2) Is it adequate? Can you live by this view? My former conservative apologetics *failed* both tests. Did it deal with all the facts? It often didn't deal with the facts that we have learned from modern scholarship in historiography, natural science, Biblical criticism, psychology, and anthropology. For example, I can no longer shut my eyes to all that we have learned about the contextual character of language. Is it sufficient to declare that God is the Lord of language and proceed to treat Biblical language as functioning differently from ordinary language? In previous Christian history some Christians contended that the Holy Ghost spoke a special kind of Greek, too. That was before we learned that the New Testament was written in *koinē*, the language of the people. God *could* create a special language, or use language in a special way. But do we need to claim that he has done so? He has apparently been willing to have the common language of humans used in ordinary ways to communicate his message.

Is purely conservative apologetic adequate? Can we live by it? I feel that I was asking people to live in a conservative ghetto. A consistently conservative position essentially demands that we be separate from the world. But Christians are called on to live "in" the world. We can benefit by all that behavioral sciences have taught us about the ways persons function in the cultures they create. We are not to be "of" the world. We should derive our values, purposes, and goals from Scripture. Then we need to accept the freedom and responsibility of evangelical Christians to challenge and change the world by preaching and living the gospel in it.

Conclusions

God is gracious. He uses weak, fallible, and hung-up sinners to do his work. I'm grateful for that. Otherwise he could never use me. Wherever the gospel is preached and Christian witness is given, the Spirit can use it. This is true no matter how mistaken or wrongly motivated it may be, or how misguidedly it is done. I thank God for the good he brings even out of the methods I least like.

At the same time, method does have consequences. If we can, we should avoid creating problems. Some methods that work as means to bring people to Christ can be stifling to their growth as Christians. I'm deeply concerned about two aspects of certain styles of apologetics. First, I'm concerned about the method of dichotomy. This method implies that either you do things my way, or you aren't doing Christian work at all. This method is given an absolute character, since it depends on absolutes. Therefore it divides Christians who need to be working together. It can also damage our witness. A zealous young Christian said to me: "I've felt that I had to tell my friends that everything they think is false. That really turns them off." Second, I'm concerned about giving false or inadequate reasons for Christian belief. This sets up young Christians for greater problems later. That happens if you claim to be able to prove the unprovable. Many sincere Christians feel they must provide profound philosophical proofs. But they know in their hearts they aren't capable of it. If we assert that the authority of Scripture and the truth about our Savior is founded on those proofs, we predispose some Christians for a terrible fall. Some will finally admit the fallacy of their supposedly infallible foundation. I know persons who were the strongest conservative evangelical Christians and had all the answers, but who have now rejected the faith altogether. To ask every Christian witness to do what even the greatest philosophers can't do is to doom them to defeat. Other people feel they must live their lives in a conservative ghetto and avoid the problems. They become dependent on our authority, our theories, our conclusions. This they do at great cost to themselves and their witness.

I've tried to say honestly where I am, and how I got here. I don't claim universal validity for my conclusions. I've set them in the context of my experience because that is a way their meaning can be understood. I don't claim to have proved my points. I have simply given my witness. I ask that you compare my experience with your own. I ask that we study Scripture together prayerfully, openly, and with all the scholarship available to us. I believe with John Robinson, a leader of the Pilgrims, that for me, for all of us, God has "yet more light to break forth from His Word."

Looking Ahead

A better understanding of faith and knowledge than Kant's will be developed by going beyond him. Ignoring Kant or going back to a pre-Kantian rationalism or empiricism is of no long-range help to Christians. The best theologians and apologists have always combined an understanding of Christian tradition with the most up-to-date conceptual thinking. I want to conserve the Augustinian understanding of the wholeness of knowledge—faith which leads to understanding. True reason, "right reason," from Augustine through Calvin and Ramus to Westminster evidenced two features which both rationalism and empiricism lack. First, knowing the truth (facts) and doing the good (values) were always inseparable. Second, the only knowledge (objective) worthy of the name "truth" was saving knowledge (subjective) that transformed a person's life. Theory and practice were not analyzed as particular stages but understood in a personal synthesis. Some contemporary humanistic psychologists, missionary anthropologists, and philosophers of ordinary language are offering new and better conceptual frameworks to help us recover a holistic understanding of truth. These are the areas in which I want to do further work as an apologist. We can conserve the best of our past by using the best of our present knowledge. Then we are evangelical apologists—offering good news—for now.

CHAPTER 11

Continuing
in Christ's Word

I have shared the preceding chapters, in mimeographed form, with several hundred people. Reactions have varied. Some said they were helped. That gratified me. Others misunderstood what I was trying to say. That grieved me. I've tried to correct those misunderstandings where I could. Still others have flatly disagreed. Always they have done so graciously. In some cases we've had to agree to disagree, in love. But in no case was there less understanding or less strong relationship as Christian persons when we had a chance to discuss our differences. Those experiences have heartened me to risk this publication. I have not been as precise and correct as I could have been if I had spent more months or years refining my stance. But I'm satisfied that I will learn more by turning this loose and listening for the response of others than by holding on to it. I am eager for creative dialogue more than I am concerned to make a careful defense. The important thing is that we take the issues very seriously. And we must not take ourselves too seriously!

People have often asked me: "Don't you think that it was good that you began conservatively? Don't you have to react to an extreme position in order to grow?" Those are good questions. I have reflected on them a lot. My first instinct is to agree. Certainly I have benefited much from the strengths of my early rigidity. I had a clear standard for comparison and change. But recently I have begun to question that premise. I have come to know people who are healthy, balanced, and orthodox and who never began from the constricting guilts and legalisms which I took on myself. Furthermore, my clinical psychologist friends contend that the movement from conservative to open is not a necessary sequence. The great achievers did not necessarily succeed because of reaction to their pasts. Indeed, the less hung up we are, the more creative we can be. I hope that is so. I'm beginning to believe it. The Bible, especially in Jesus, suggests that model. And we are to follow him.

Avoiding the Dilemma

It is possible to avoid the extremes of both conservatism and liberalism and yet develop into an outstanding evangelical theologian. My example is G. C. Berkouwer of the Netherlands. I've spoken about his initial impact on me. I want to indicate directions I think he continues to point for us. You could suggest other viable candidates. I use Berkouwer as an example because it was my great privilege to study with him and to have personal contact with him over a period of eight years.

Berkouwer is a product of his past. He has maintained continuity with his own orthodox Dutch Reformed tradition while making creative application of it to new problems. What intrigues me is the difference between the evangelical tradition in the Netherlands and its counterpart in this country. Berkouwer's great predecessors in the chair of dogmatics at the Free University were Abraham Kuyper and Herman Bavinck.

(Valentine Hepp came between Bavinck and Berkouwer, but his scholasticism exercised no discernible influence on Berkouwer or the Reformed tradition.) Like Kuyper and Bavinck, Berkouwer combines Calvinism and humane learning, piety and social conscience, with no apparent sense of tension. Kuyper had built into the Dutch tradition a concern that Christianity pervade every sphere of life. It was when Kuyper became prime minister of the Netherlands that Bavinck succeeded him as professor of dogmatics. Bavinck's four-volume *Reformed Dogmatics* became the standard work out of which Berkouwer's theology was formed and to which he continually refers. It is fascinating to reflect that Bavinck was a contemporary of B. B. Warfield. They knew and respected each other as evangelical colleagues. Yet the styles of their theologies and their practical effects were very different. Warfield left on his followers the imprint of the apologist and polemicist. Bavinck influenced the generations after him to be theological scientists and churchmen. Berkouwer reflects this influence. Withal, he is warm and human. I came to his study one day to take an exam. It happened that he asked me how a fellow American student was coming in his work. I rather self-righteously replied that I had observed my friend playing tennis that morning. Berkouwer's gentle reply was: "Life is more than science!" The human and the scholarly always enhance each other in Berkouwer's approach.

Evangelical Authority

For American conservative evangelicals the central point of concern has always been the doctrine of Scripture. I have made it the special focus of my theological study since seminary days. At the Free University I sensed a different orientation. So, I wrote my Th.M. thesis on Herman Bavinck's concept of "organic inspiration." I assisted in translating and editing Berkouwer's two volumes on Holy Scripture for publication in one volume in English. I believe that this work on Scripture really does break the liberal-conservative dilemmas we have wrestled with for a century. It conserves the basic thrust of the Reformers and it liberates us from unfruitful old orientations. It offers a genuinely evangelical middle way.

Berkouwer wrote an early book on Scripture. It encourages me to see how his thinking has changed and developed in this mature work. But a basic evangelical principle was foundational from the beginning. The extremes—formalism and subjectivism, rationalism and existentialism—have been rejected. We do not have to choose one or the other of those extremes as so much of our American theology has suggested.

Faith, Not Theory

Theology is a product of faith. All theological statements should be statements which a believer can make in faith. No theory about the nature of Scripture guarantees its authority. A willing subjection to the Bible's authority in my life is what matters. We are on common ground when we acknowledge our personal commitment to the authority of the Bible. Then we are ready to discuss what theories about the Bible are most adequate to describe it. Our faith doesn't depend on the theories. The theories are ways that persons of faith try to understand their commitment. We accept the Bible with the same faith we have in Christ who is its center. Then we can honestly face all the difficult questions without fear! When Berkouwer returned from being an official observer at the Second Vatican

Council he was criticized by some members of his church. At a press conference one reporter asked: "Don't you think that participation in the Council is a dangerous thing?" Berkouwer's reply was characteristic. "Danger," he said, "is not a theological word."

In the nineteenth century, while Hodge and Warfield were building defenses against Biblical criticism, Kuyper and Bavinck were meeting the issue openly and constructively. It is highly significant that Bavinck quotes Kuyper only once in his *Reformed Dogmatics*. That quotation indicates the unity of their approach to critical questions. Kuyper wrote:

> If in the four Gospels, words are put in the mouth of Jesus on the same occasion which are dissimilar in form of expression, Jesus naturally cannot have used four forms at the same time, but the Holy Spirit only intended to create an impression for the Church which perfectly answers to what went out from Jesus.

What a beautiful and sensible statement! We are to listen for the message of Scripture. All the overly elaborate and unconvincing efforts to find a rational answer to every apparent problem in Scripture are relegated to scholarship. Our faith doesn't depend on their resolution. This attitude is possible because the Dutch Reformed tradition, like Calvin, grounds our acceptance of the Bible's authority in the testimony of the Holy Spirit in our hearts. All the evidences of the Bible's truth and value are encouragements and supports to the believer. But our faith does not depend on logically sufficient evidence. If it did, only scholars could believe. Or else we would all believe on the testimony of the scholars rather than on the testimony of the Spirit in our own experience with the Word.

Content, Not Form

The hardest problem for us as conservative evangelicals to handle has been alleged errors in the Bible. Berkouwer returns to the Biblical notion of error. Biblically, error is not wrong understanding by the mind. Biblically, error is stubborn resistance from the heart. To err is to miss the mark, to fail to acknowledge the point of Scripture. Error involves rejecting the content of the Bible. A racist can proclaim that he believes in the historical and scientific veracity of every word in the Bible. But he will still be very much in error from a Biblical viewpoint.

A central concern for proving the objective historical and scientific accuracy is a nineteenth-century development. You have probably seen, as I have, graphs indicating that 90 percent of all the scientists who have ever lived are still living. Science as we know it is modern, not ancient. And culturally the Bible is Eastern, not Western. There is no way that we can ignore these factors without denying the human character of the Bible. Denial of the temporal and cultural conditioning of the Bible can have disastrous effects on hearing its central message. It led, for example, to the attempted Biblical legitimation of slavery. When we fasten on the form in which the Biblical data are given we risk missing the content. God's revelation was given to specific people in particular times and places. To sanctify the time and place is sometimes to miss the point.

We all concede that translation of Scripture is necessary. The message given in one form must be transferred to another form. But it is the same message. God didn't create a supernatural language and insist that we all learn it before we could hear him. He communicated through the common language of every people to whom he spoke. And he continues to speak through Bible translations in 1,526 different human languages. Sometimes the Biblical words and images simply don't exist in other languages. Every translation of the Scriptures is also an interpretation. And yet, God's saving message comes through to people in their own tongue. That's what counts. What Jesus means by understanding Scripture is accepting its saving message in our hearts. To the Pharisees, who knew all the words, he said: "You search the scriptures, because you think that in them you have eternal life; and it is they that bear witness to me" (John 5:39).

Bavinck repeatedly stated that since the Scripture is writing it is subject to the fate of all writing. The general rules of interpretation that apply to all literary work must be applied to Scripture as well. Our assessment of the literary character of a work is quite different from our feelings about its truth and value. It is impossible to come to the Scripture without any presuppositions. As Christians we should come with the bias of faith. That faith is in the normativity of the Bible's message for us. And we should be as honest and self-critical of our other biases as we can. Pure objectivity isn't possible. A controlled subjectivity is our goal. For that we need to listen to others. They can help us to hear what our biases have blocked.

For the Reformers, all the characteristics of Scripture—its authority, reliability, clarity, and sufficiency—were characteristics of its content, not its form. Erasmus argued against Luther that because of problems in the form of Scripture we should simply obey the church. Luther admitted problems with the words, but contended that the issues, the contents, were clear. Calvin discusses an inaccuracy in Paul's quotation of Ps. 51:4 in Rom. 3:4, and he is led to generalize:

> We indeed know that the Apostles in quoting Scripture often used a freer language than the original; for they counted it enough to quote what was suitable to their subject: hence they made no great account of words. (Commentary on Romans 3:4.)

In another place Calvin notes that God's method of communication is "to represent himself to us, not as he is in himself, but as he seems to us" (*Institutes* I. xvii. 13). Berkouwer's tradition reaches back to the Reformers in its deep concern for the saving content of Scripture. That content comes in ancient, Near Eastern forms that are sometimes very different from our contemporary, Western ones.

Biblical words are not only written—they are spoken. The apostles preached before they wrote. That oral preaching was written so that it would not perish. Preaching continues to be the Word of God. The Second Helvetic Confession, Ch. I, proclaims the Reformers' view that "The Preaching of the Word of God is the Word of God." Whether a person addresses a congregation from a pulpit or speaks to a friend in private—if the Biblical message is communicated, the Word of God has been proclaimed.

Certainty and Salvation

We don't have to choose between critical judgment and the certainty of faith. Certainty lies not in the theoretical but the practical realm. Faith gives us certainty. Then we are free to use our critical intelligence on all the facts. Sometimes we conservative evangelicals have used the incarnation of the divine and human natures in Christ as an analogy for Scripture. We must be careful of such analogies. The incarnation of God in human form in Jesus Christ is unique. To be sure, like

Christ, Scripture is both divine and human. But only Christ was sinless. We worship Christ. But we instinctively recognize that worshiping the Bible is illegitimate. Christology is a central doctrine. Bibliolatry is a heresy.

The final dilemma which Berkouwer rejects is that between salvation and service. In the gospel they are woven together. So are the rights of the individual and the responsibilities of the corporate body. Individualism has gone wrong when it becomes egotism. And social service is corrupted when it serves to feed the ego or to assuage the guilt of the doer—individual or corporate. Jesus said: "If you continue in my word, you are truly my disciples, and you will know the truth, and the truth will make you free" (John 8:31–32). That statement is surely another way of saying: "If any man's will is to do his will, he shall know whether the teaching is from God" (John 7:17).

The Evangelical Center

G. C. Berkouwer has taught that the choice between conservatism and liberalism is a false dilemma. He has taught this by the irenic manner of his life as well as by his thought. He has always sought the good in each person and situation. His denomination was not a member of the World Council of Churches, but it chose him to go as observer to the New Delhi assembly of that body. Berkouwer preached for me before the Pilgrim Fellowship in Dordrecht the day before he left for New Delhi. His presentation both amazed and disappointed our American worshipers. He entered the pulpit with only a six-inch square of paper on which were scribbled a few words. He preached and prayed in masterful English. His prayer came from a heart filled with love for all members of the body of Christ and heavy with his own sense of responsibility. The worshipers were disappointed by his sermon. They could understand it! They expected the great professor to be profound (i.e., abstract, dull). Instead, he preached a simple gospel sermon of pastoral comfort and affirmation. For Berkouwer, theology is always and only the servant of the church. Theology is good only if it can be preached! Berkouwer also went as a designated observer to the Second Vatican Council and to a meeting of the International Council of Christian Churches. At the latter meeting he was personally attacked from the platform. Yet when he reported each of these situations his favorite text of Scripture remained II Tim. 2:9. Paul has just described his situation of suffering and wearing fetters like a criminal. But he proclaims: "The word of God is not bound." Berkouwer contends that as long as we read the same Bible with conservatives or liberals, Catholics or sectarians, we can't predict the outcome. God's Spirit will work through his Word.

Conservatives and progressives (Berkouwer's term) can both turn to Scripture for support. There are many texts that admonish us to conserve the best of the past (e.g., I Tim. 6:20; II Tim. 3:14; Heb. 13:8). Jeremiah urged his hearers to seek the ancient paths (Jer. 6:16). Progressives seeking change can find precedents as well. "The old has passed away, behold, the new has come" (II Cor. 5:17). New wine demands fresh wineskins to hold it (Mark 2:22). The Pharisees who held fast to the old law couldn't see the new Messianic fulfillment.

Equally relevant as any of those texts are those which speak of the unity of the body of Christ. Paul wrote: "Is Christ divided?" (I Cor. 1:13.) And Calvin is said to have commented: "If Christ is divided, who bleeds?" Christ prayed that his disciples might be one—that the world might believe (John 17:21). Our lives as Christians are defined by our love and concern for one another (I Cor. 12:25; I John 3:18).

All dilemmas between past and future orientations are overcome in Phil. 3:12–16. Paul sounds the most liberal, change-oriented note by saying that he is "forgetting what lies behind and straining forward to what lies ahead." But he closes with a conservative footnote: "Only let us hold true to what we have attained." The past is crucial because God has come into that past to make all things new in Jesus Christ.

Conservatives are not wrong for trying to preserve continuity. Problems arise through our inadequate views of *how* this is to be done. For Berkouwer, truth is not isolated in doctrine, but is that in which we must *walk*. We are exhorted not only to hearing and keeping (Luke 11:28) but *also* to hearing and *doing* (Luke 8:21). An orthodoxy of words without deeds is not truly orthodox. The Biblical concern is whether we are walking in the truth (II John 4; III John 3, 4). The gospel is the power of God unto salvation—personal and social—now, not just in the past (Rom. 1:16). We will find resources in the gospel tradition that we have faithfully conserved. We must use those resources to meet every present and future problem. To do that, we need all the resources of the body of Christ. We need one another.

How can we best help one another? Berkouwer has chosen one way. All his life he has patiently worked at central theological problems. He has taken issues one at a time and brought massive scholarly resources to bear on them. He has listened to, and held private discussions with, theologians of other traditions, learning from them and contributing to their thought. Slowly he has developed a scholarly, pastoral, evangelical stance. And he has brought a whole denomination with him. That denomination, The Reformed Churches in the Netherlands, began in rather conservative isolation and now has symbolized its more open stance by joining the World Council of

Churches. G. C. Berkouwer and the Gereformeerde Kerken have had influence disproportionate to their size. Berkouwer's way has been a good way, and many have benefited from it.

The United States and Holland are, of course, different. Evangelicals in this country come from a startling variety of traditions. My theological education and early teaching were all in Reformed institutions. Yet at Fuller Seminary the first time I began, "Calvin says," half the class winced! And within each of our denominational traditions there are varieties of theological orientations. The United States is a pluralistic society. The church in the United States is multifaceted. How then are we to hear and help each other? We need to know our own traditions well. But we cannot afford just to conserve them at all costs. That would be idolizing the works of men.

My response to pluralism has been personal. I can tell you how I have experienced the grace of God. I have tried to say how I have learned and grown. The struggles have been more severe, the doubts more difficult than I have been able to capture in writing. I don't want to alienate old comrades. I want to affirm their contributions to my life. I also seek new friends and new understanding. But this is the choice I have made: to reveal something of myself. I've taken the risk of thinking out loud. I hope that it will encourage you to do the same. I think we in the conservative evangelical community have commonality and confidence enough to be able to afford open discussion. By revealing ourselves and openly discussing our differences we begin to be ready to love each other at deeper levels than before. Such openness to issues and to other persons can be frightening for all of us. But, praise God, love casts out fear (I John 4:18). That is the good news, the gospel, the evangel. At least it is good news for this one emerging evangelical.